Doris Collins, the you
when her mother was fo
Cooper by name and a r

She began developi
despite the demands of
and then several years of running a hotel in Worthing, she
has been involved in psychic work and healing for over
forty years.

She has conducted demonstrations before huge
audiences in Britain, the United States, Australia, New
Zealand, South Africa and Europe, and has also worked
successfully through radio phone-in programmes.

G000167858

By the same author
A Woman of Spirit

DORIS COLLINS

The Power Within

GRAFTON BOOKS

A Division of the Collins Publishing Group

LONDON GLASGOW
TORONTO SYDNEY AUCKLAND

Grafton Books
A Division of the Collins Publishing Group
8 Grafton Street, London W1X 3LA

Published by Grafton Books 1987

First published in Great Britain by
Grafton Books 1986

Copyright © Doris Collins 1986

ISBN 0-586-06816-3

Printed and bound in Great Britain by
Collins, Glasgow

Set in Times

CONTENTS

'I must have no hatred or
bitterness for anyone'
EDITH CAVELL

I should like to thank my literary agent
Jeffrey Simmons without whose help this
book could not have been written

CHAPTER 1

The Written Word

The telephone rang at an unwanted moment. I had not long returned from a tiring eight-week tour of Australia and New Zealand, following publication of my first book, and I was sitting quietly at home, talking to a newspaper reporter who had come to interview me about my trip. I lifted the receiver automatically, intending to ask my caller to ring back later.

'Hullo, mum,' a man said in a voice quite unfamiliar to me, 'this is Richard.'

I did not at first make the connection and thought that someone was playing a joke or that he had the wrong number.

'Mum,' he said when I did not reply, 'this is your son, Richard Collins.'

I have heard people say 'You could have knocked me down with a feather' but I am rather a large person and did not ever think it could happen to me.

As readers of *A Woman of Spirit* will remember, I have two stepsons. My second husband had two sons by his first marriage, and the younger boy Richard was a dwarf. I make no distinction between children and stepchildren and he was as dear to me as my own children, but I had lost track of him since he joined Chipperfield's Circus and went with them to South Africa, from which – as far as I knew – he had never returned.

He had a Bohemian nature and wanted to be free and succeed in life on his own account. Whether he felt that I was too much of a restraining influence on him or that his independence was threatened in our family environment, I have often speculated; but in any case we did not hear from him and I felt to some extent that I had lost a loved one.

This worried me a great deal over the years and when I first went to South Africa I tried to find him. I thought that because he was a dwarf, it would be easy to locate him, and I daresay that if I had been a detective I would have done so, but all my efforts came to naught and I did not in any case have the time to make exhaustive enquiries. I tried to find him psychically too, but the psychic gift is one that cannot always be turned on and off at will, particularly in matters where one is personally concerned, and all I was able to deduce in this way was that he was somewhere in the Cape Town area. I returned home a disappointed woman. None of the family ever forgot him – we often talked about him and wondered how he was getting on – but he had disappeared completely from our sight, if not from our minds.

I had not heard from him for over twenty years and now here he was on the telephone as if we had never been apart. I cannot tell you what it meant to me suddenly to hear his voice again. I was quite overcome with emotion and wished that the reporter were not there. In retrospect I am very glad that he was there, because he published a report of what happened; and as readers of my first book will know, I try never to write anything that cannot be supported by independent evidence.

The reporter wrote that he saw a different side of me for the first time. Few people realise that I have a very emotional side to me. I cannot show it too obviously because so much of my work involves other people's emotions, and if I myself become upset, my own feelings will communicate themselves to the people I am trying to help. It is no good if a surgeon's hand shakes because he is about to operate on a friend. In the same way, I have to be personally involved but almost clinically aloof if I am to operate successfully. The only criticism that has ever been made of my work is that I sometimes appear a little bit tough in the way I handle people, but I assure you that, if indeed that is so, it is a necessary buffer against excessive emotionalism that would be counter-productive.

Hearing my lost son's voice was almost like being stabbed. It actually hurt for a moment.

I was so confused that I said one of the silliest things anybody could possibly say: 'You sound like a man.'

'I am a man,' he said. 'I am nearly forty years old.'

Of course he was. My mind went back to the time when I married his father. Richard was only four and I tried to bring him up to do everything everybody else could do, despite his size. He was a difficult child and I did not always have an easy time with him. He now reminded me that I had taught him to be independent and to stand on his own two feet. 'I want to thank you, Mother, for making me tough,' he said.

I was near to tears as I tried to talk to him. 'How did you find me?' I asked.

He told me that he was now happily married in South Africa, living in Cape Town, and that he had had a son and daughter of his own. Unfortunately he had lost the little girl, whom he had named Doris after me, but he had a wonderful boy called Ricky. He made a point of telling me that Ricky was quite normal. 'Of course he is,' I said. I had always brought Richard up to accept himself as normal, although he was a dwarf. The world can be a very hard place for anyone who is different, and I tried never to make him feel that he was different.

He had made a big success in business and one day his secretary asked him whether his mother's name was Doris Collins. She told him that she had read a book by someone of that name in which the author mentioned a dwarf son called Richard. She naturally thought that the author might be his mother.

He immediately read the book and telephoned the publishers in London, who put him on to my literary agent, who in turn gave him my number. His call took me quite off balance, as you might expect after such a long time, and it incidentally gave the reporter a better story than the one he had come about. Richard invited me to visit him and his wife, and of course that is something I am really looking forward to as soon as I get the opportunity.

As soon as I put down the phone, I apologised to the reporter and telephoned my other son, who was very excited by my news. 'Did you tell him,' he asked, 'that his father is dead?'

'No, I didn't,' I replied. 'It was all too quick.'

That evening I discussed matters with my husband and we decided to telephone Richard in Cape Town. 'We didn't speak,' I said, 'about your father.'

'There was no need, Mother,' he pointed out. 'I know he died. I read your book!'

I should have thought of that and I felt a bit foolish for a moment, but then he said something very wonderful to me indeed. 'I want to tell you,' he said, 'that I never knew my own mother. She died before I could remember her and to me you have always been my mother. I want to thank you very much for making me a man.'

Those few words were the recompense for all the difficulties I had had with Richard as a child. They made everything one hundred per cent worth while.

I have worked in my field for almost half a century but the urge to communicate my experiences to a worldwide audience did not begin to build up until four or five years ago. Something told me that I ought to write a book but I never quite knew why. Now, following my lost son's telephone call, I thought perhaps that one of the reasons was to bring my family together. I have also been put in touch with two first cousins, daughters of one of my mother's brothers who contacted me after reading my book.

I had always realised the power of words and the power of

thought, which is only silent words after all, but until I wrote a book I had not fully realised the extraordinary power of the written word. It has opened up a whole new world to me, and I can hardly believe the number of letters I have received from all corners of the globe from people who have read my book and are interested in my work. People have a very great need for inner peace, and of course for good health, and so many correspondents have indicated that my book has helped them in some way.

My work has not changed but so many more people have become aware of what I do, both through the book and through the widespread public appearances I have been making as a result of the book's success. There is a pattern in everything, and I can see now that the book was part of a particular pattern.

When I had the urge to write, I did not know how to go about it. I had demonstrated clairvoyance and healing before large audiences over the years and I had never been lost for words. I was also quite a practised public speaker. But that is not the same thing as being able to write a book. I did not believe that it was simply a question of talking into a machine and transcribing my words. In fact I made a couple of starts on the book unsuccessfully.

I told my dear friend and supporter, Michael Bentine, that I doubted if I would bother after all to write a book. It was he who had encouraged me so strongly to do so. 'You must,' he said, 'and I'll introduce you to someone who will help you to get over your mental block.'

Some short time later I found myself sitting next to Michael's literary agent at a dinner party at the Bentines'. I told him about myself and the book I wanted to write, and I was pleased, and somewhat surprised, when he reacted favourably. In fact he offered to try to sell the book to a publisher.

'Before a word is written?' I asked.

'In your case, yes,' he said. 'I'll take you along to a publisher and you just tell him what you've told me.'

'But I can't write,' I protested. 'I've tried.'

I was highly amused by his reply. 'If you can talk,' he said, 'you can write. In fact if I'd recorded what you have been saying, it could almost go into a book as it stands.'

I did not tell him that when I had tried to do things that way, it had not worked.

Even as he was speaking, I knew that he would find a publisher for me and that the book would be written. I am much better at seeing things for other people than for myself, but I was suddenly sure of success, and I said so. He laughed and told me he would get in touch with me as soon as possible.

I did not have to wait long. He contacted me sooner than expected to say that he had made an appointment for me to see not one publisher, but two – at the same time. I was too surprised to ask any questions, and I merely arranged to meet the agent at his office and to go with him, wherever he wanted to take me.

It was a day I shall not forget in a hurry because of the foul weather. I struggled up to town through the thick February snow that was playing havoc with the traffic, arriving at the agent's almost a half-hour late. We could not find a taxi and waited for what seemed an age for a bus. The agent reassured me by saying, 'Things that begin badly have a habit of ending well.' It was only then that he told me the names of the people to whom he would introduce me and the name of the publishing company we were on the way to visit.

We were of course late for our appointment. Worse still, we were soaked through. Even my practical boots were no match for the snow. Everybody was very kind, however. We were not the only latecomers that day and we were allowed to thaw out and were given a hot drink before being shown into an office where two men were sitting.

My agent had set up a meeting with the company's senior hardback and paperback editors at the same time. We met in the hardback editor's office and I felt completely at home. He was such a charming man and I was immediately drawn to him. The other gentleman was equally charming but seemed more aloof.

I felt very comfortable for some reason, although this was an entirely new world to me. I hardly heard what my agent was saying. I am sure he said all the right things but my mind was elsewhere. Without warning, I interrupted his flow. He looked at me rather uncertainly but let me speak, and suddenly I was telling the paperback editor all about his first wife, the break-up of his marriage, the difference between his first and second wife and personal matters of that sort.

His secretary came into the room to say that there was a telephone call for him from America, so he went into his own office to take it. As soon as he had gone, the hardback editor said: 'What you told him was absolutely accurate. It's quite amazing. But what on earth made you do so?'

'It's just that I thought he was less interested in the book than you were,' I replied.

The two men in the room, my agent and the publisher, fell about laughing. The following day the agent rang up to say that the publishers had offered him a contract at his asking price.

The book seemed to write itself as if it was on oiled wheels. My main purpose in writing it was not to tell the story of my life, or to seek personal publicity, but to explain my work as a healer and a psychic. I know from the letters I have received that the proof I have given of survival after death has brought great comfort to many of my readers, and that is principally why I am so pleased that the book sold very well both in hardback and in paperback and that I have been asked to write this second volume.

Following publication of the first book, I was asked to appear up and down the country. I had been holding occasional meetings for many years, but not on a regular or highly organised basis. One night, when I was appearing at the theatre in Camden Town in London, my literary agent brought a friend along to see me. She was the remarkable lady who had managed Lulu's career so successfully since the singer was a child of fifteen. She came backstage afterwards and told me that she believed in my work as a clairvoyant and healer. She had considerable experience of the psychic world and had seen a number of clairvoyants at work, but no one had impressed her more than I.

I later learnt that, although she had been approached to manage many other artists, both famous and unknown, she had decided that looking after Lulu was as much as she wanted to do. Not knowing this, I had an immediate feeling that she would take me under her wing. I also knew that I wanted to reach a wider audience, not for any selfish or monetary reason, but because I honestly felt that my book had given me an opportunity to prove survival and the power of healing to a bigger audience than ever before. It turned out that this lady saw in me a challenge that interested her, and she offered to help to promote a series of personal appearances by me throughout the country. Finally it was agreed that I would hold two trial meetings in Scotland, one each in Irvine and Lochgelly. Perhaps it was thought that if I made a mess of things, it was better to do so as far away from London as possible!

First, however, I had to return to Australia where, as a result of local interest in my book, the major television show *Sixty Minutes* put out a programme about me, having helped to organise an eight-week tour for me that took me to Melbourne, Adelaide, Hobart, Canberra, Brisbane and Sydney. I also flew over to New Zealand for two days to try to help a girl who had been harmed because of some sort of involvement with what I can only call the occult. I gave her healing and, I hope, some good and helpful advice.

The visit to Australia was really exhausting, not least because I was constantly under the microscope. *Sixty Minutes* wanted to confront me with a man who had made a reputation for himself as a disbeliever in spiritualism, but I refused to appear on a platform with him – I had no objection of course to him appearing separately – because I felt that his destructive efforts might adversely affect the atmosphere in which I operated. I was also monitored by an organisation calling itself Australian Sceptics, who actually put out a do-it-yourself clairvoyancy kit, if you can believe it, that sold for two dollars. I told them that when people try to destroy things, it comes back to them like a boomerang, and I simply got on with my work. I believe I gave as good as I took, but in any case I am not over-concerned with what people say and think. I prefer them to think well of me, but everyone is entitled to an opinion and I know what I am doing and I have a clear conscience about it.

I prefer the testimony of the many people I healed and to whom I brought comfort, as for example the woman whose young son came to me with a message for his mother towards the end of my biggest meeting in Australia. According to reports in the newspapers, I almost vomited on stage. 'It's given me a very sick feeling,' I am quoted as saying. 'I wanted to bring fluid up then. I apologise but I can't help that. When the spirits touch me, I can't help how I react.' Apparently this impressed the audience more than almost anything else, but of course they probably may not have realised how physically a medium can be involved with someone who has a message from the other side. A man who has hanged himself may, for example, seize my rope of pearls, if I am wearing it. In fact his action becomes part of the shorthand by which I understand how he came by his death.

One thing I did in Australia was to contact Pamela Morrison. She is the half-sister of Roy Stockdill, deputy features editor of the *News of the World*. Roy is a delightful man but he is what you might call a hard-bitten journalist, not given to fanciful speculation. Indeed, as he himself declared when he wrote this story in his newspaper, he is a natural sceptic. But he was shaken, he admits, by an extraordinary personal experience while he was researching a series that the newspaper was planning about the paranormal.

For forty years he had believed that he was an only child, but when he started to trace his family history, he was startled to find that his father had had a daughter called Pamela, who was born three years before him. She had been taken to Scotland to live with relations as a small child, and Roy now decided against trying to find her in case it caused her distress. In fact he almost forgot about her until he met me, during the course of his research, at a spiritualist meeting in Wimbledon. I told him that I had a message from his mother, who had died just over a year before, concerning his sister. 'She's telling me about your sister,' I said, 'that she took your name. Your mother is saying to me, "Tell him it's all right, she does belong."'

Two days later he flew to Edinburgh on business and decided to use a spare hour or two looking through official records. He discovered that his half-sister had been married twice, but each time in the name of Pamela Stockdill. This proved to him that the message I had given him that she had taken his name was correct.

Five days later he received a letter, written on the very day he had been in Edinburgh, from New South Wales, Australia. It was from the sister he had never met and whose existence he had not even known about until recently. 'It has taken me twenty years,' she wrote, 'to get enough courage to write this. I was always scared of rejection or causing trouble.' She added that she had never known her father but wanted the chance to know her brother.

Roy telephoned her immediately. She said she had known about him for years but had only just plucked up courage to contact him. She was interested in the psychic world and was in fact a member of a spiritualist church. Why had she chosen that particular moment to get in touch with him when, as a result of my message from his mother, he was looking for further evidence about her? 'I just had a feeling, that's all,' she said.

Of course this episode was nothing unusual to me and was in no way surprising but I believe it affected Roy quite considerably. When I was in Australia, I took advantage of my presence there to meet his sister, now Mrs Pamela Morrison. I sent her tickets for one of my meetings and, at Roy's request, gave her a lovely bunch of flowers from him.

No sooner had I returned, somewhat exhausted, from Australia than I was whisked up to Scotland for my two meetings. There was very little time to prepare and conditions were far from ideal. It was the dead of winter and snow was thick on the ground. Both meetings, however, were very successful and every seat was sold. I agreed therefore to hold an extra meeting in each place, and then to fulfil other engagements that were hastily arranged for me on my way south.

Fortunately the promoters provided me with the most marvellous chauffeur, who removed a tremendous burden from my shoulders by making arrangements on my behalf and seeing I got to my destinations in good time. He was actually much more than a driver. In fact I called him my road manager because he did so very much more to help me than just drive me from place to place. I had to laugh when I was criticised for riding about in a limousine with a bodyguard, as if I was a gangster. How else could I have managed to get everywhere on time? It is a big responsibility to appear in public, and I could not do it on my own. There has to be back-up, and I needed the help of other people just as one might need the help of a lawyer or a plumber. If I were content to preach to the converted, I would not need much assistance, but I was seeking a wider public and I needed to present myself professionally.

My minder's name was Keith. He had had a lot of experience with pop stars but I think I was a very different proposition for him. He had never known anyone like me, and I am sure at first he thought my work was a whole lot of rubbish. Right at the start however something happened that convinced him that my gifts were genuine. We were in Lochgelly when he expressed the view that the deputy manager of the theatre, whom he knew well, might be very sceptical about clairvoyance. There was a fifteen-minute interval during the meeting and I was having a cup of tea backstage when the deputy manager walked in. I saw a little boy at his side, aged about two and a half, and I knew at once that he was the man's son and that he had died of leukaemia. Among other things, the child gave me his name and indicated that his father had a photograph of him in his wallet which he looked at frequently and even spoke to. The boy told me that he had a sister called Sarah and that while he had been in hospital, the doctor had given him a little toy dog that he had called Handy, which was the doctor's surname. He also had a dog at home called Spit, which I thought was an unusual name.

I am always very loath to talk to people about personal matters except in the course of my work. At the time I was resting during the interval, but I felt impelled to tell the father what his son was saying to me. It appears that it was all true. I do not know what effect this had on the father but it certainly convinced Keith that my gift was genuine.

I tried in the first book never to make claims that could not be substantiated by independent evidence. This was not always easy because I had not kept careful records. For the purpose of this new book, however, I have been at pains to record as much as possible, and in particular I have tape-recordings of all that happened during the early part of 1985 when I appeared nightly in theatres up and down the country. I believe that this constitutes a unique body of evidence of survival after death, and it is supported by newspaper reports of my meetings. I am not of course fully aware of what is happening while I am working on stage and I have been able for the first time, through this documentation, to analyse my work for myself.

I have been appearing on platforms all my adult life but it is another matter entirely to fill a huge theatre. I have done that too on many occasions, but not night after night for a whole month or more, with only a break on Sunday. The responsibility was awesome, although I did not realise it at the time. I had to give a different performance every night because I never knew who would come to me, or with what messages.

An actress learns her play by heart and every move is planned. In any case she is part of a company. If she forgets her lines, there is someone to prompt her. If she falls ill, she has an understudy to play her role. But there was no one to understudy me, and if I dried up there was no show. People who had bought tickets would have to be given their money back.

During February 1985 I made twenty separate appearances, and so great was the response that I agreed, in a
moment akin to something like madness, to fulfil a further
twenty-six engagements in twenty-eight days in April and
May. I must continue this work – and arrangements have
been made for me to do so – but I shall never agree again to
such a concentrated programme, which was far too exhausting. The promoter at least recognised this when he gave me
a golden disc for what he called a mammoth tour.

Naturally everybody wanted me because I could fill
theatres, and there were sometimes even overflow crowds. I
do not want to sound too boastful but, following my success
at the box office, one or two other psychics tried to copy my
example but found that they were playing to almost empty
houses. I do not know why that should be, but it is a fact. No
one before me had ever appeared in so many places in such
a short time. My friend Doris Stokes was one of the first to go
out and do a big tour, but most people did perhaps two or
three nights at most and then had a break. In my case it was
almost non-stop. Fortunately I have a strong constitution
and I sleep well, so I am usually fully recovered by the next
day, but it was only after it was all over that I realised what
a lot the tour had taken out of me. It has, however, provided
me with a great deal of evidence for this new book.

But for the success of my first book, I am sure that my
'theatrical' work would not have flourished so swiftly. That
is what I mean by the power of the written word.

I was not altogether happy, however, with the way some
newspapers described my appearances on stage as a competition between myself and Doris Stokes. The *Sunday Mirror*
possibly created the impression with a two-page article
under a huge banner headline: 'Battle of the Psychic
Superstars', and the *Daily Mail* asked: 'Which Doris will
win this amazing show-business battle of the mediums?' I

should really be grateful to them for the publicity that resulted in my meetings being sell-outs – in Folkestone they had to provide two hundred extra seats and the meeting in Bradford was transferred to a larger theatre – but in fact there is no animosity or enmity between Doris Stokes and me, and we each work in our own individual way. Because of the similarity of our names, some people may get us mixed up or even think that we are one and the same person, but whatever Fleet Street may print, there is no such thing as a battle of the Dorises.

Success also breeds jealousy and both Doris Stokes and I have been accused of being 'superstars', as if there is something wrong with being at the top of one's trade or profession. If being a psychic superstar means that I am now able to get my message to a larger audience, I take it as a compliment because I do not just want to preach to the converted. If it means that my head is in the clouds and that I let my imagination run away with me, I can only reply that anyone who really knows me will agree about one thing, if nothing else – I am the most practical person and my feet are very much on the ground.

The most interesting thing for me about my meetings was that more than half the audiences had never been to anything like that before. I used to ask them to indicate this by raising their hands. There were always many young people in the audiences too. The idea of a spiritualist meeting being a collection of little old ladies is absolute rubbish.

By and large, newspaper coverage of my tour was very fair, although one or two journalists hinted inevitably – but produced no evidence – that my theatre appearances were stage-managed in the sense that I had planted people in the audience and had microphones in prearranged positions, and so on. They could not have made many enquiries behind the scenes. Just tell that to the stagehands and the lighting boys, for instance, and see what they have to say.

In fact I almost had an embarrassment in Walthamstow Town Hall, which is not very far from where I was born and brought up. I need to be quite sure that nobody ever thinks I have any connection with anybody in the audience, and I would never deliberately give a message publicly to someone I knew personally. Indeed I never even open the letters that are always waiting for me until after the meetings in case people have written to say that they will be in the audience.

On this occasion a spirit came but did not actually show herself to me. She told me her name was Elsie and that she had a daughter named Linda in the hall. There were over two thousand people there but she pinpointed the girl immediately and gave me messages for her.

After the show, the girl came backstage and told me that she and her mother had lived in the same street as us and that she had been very friendly with my daughter. When she mentioned her mother's surname, I knew immediately who the lady was. She was an old friend of mine. I would never have continued with the messages if the woman had shown herself to me physically at the beginning. Had she done so, I would have recognised her and would have stopped her then and there and passed on to somebody else. I have to be very careful that people do not think that my meetings are rigged.

I find myself now, in my sixties, known to a wider public than ever before – all thanks, I believe, to my book. I will avoid as far as possible in this second book repeating things that I have said before, but to some extent it is impossible; and I ask those readers who may be familiar with a point I am making to bear with me for the sake of those who are not.

One thing I will say. Despite the strength of the evidence

I have already given of survival, I appreciate that belief requires an act of faith. If you say that you have seen a ghost, it is easy for a non-believer to say that you were dreaming or even hallucinating, and perhaps you were. But if you yourself have seen a ghost, it will be easy for you to believe that someone else may have done so.

I cannot make anyone believe. Nothing can do that. In fact sometimes the more evidence you produce, the less convincing it becomes. A jury can believe three pieces of evidence more easily than three hundred. Belief comes from within, and all I ask is that you read my words with an open mind.

CHAPTER 2

Proving Survival

When I appear on stage, we usually have one interval and devote the first session to clairvoyance and the second to healing.

The problem with healing is that its benefits cannot always be easily observed. Sufferers will know whether they feel better but an audience has to take their word for it, except on the occasions when something almost miraculous does appear to take place before their eyes. I am a clairvoyant and a healer and I use my clairvoyant abilities sometimes to help me with my healing. A man may tell me that he has a bad leg when I know clairvoyantly that the trouble stems from another part of his body.

All my work is important to me. Clairvoyance may be more theatrical in terms of an audience's experience, and I have therefore been asked to devote the entire evening to it, but I always insist on a healing session. I try to bring mental comfort to people who have lost their loved ones and physical comfort to people in pain. It is all part of the same work.

I soon learnt that I could not possibly deal with more than perhaps half a dozen people who needed healing in any one evening, and also that I had to select people whose problems could be observed to some extent by the audience. I became used to the courage of people who were really handicapped but who managed somehow to get to the theatre. Many of them were so disabled that I did not want them to have to climb the stairs to reach the stage, so I usually gave them private healing after the performance.

I have said before, but I must repeat, that I do not attempt to replace the medical profession. I shall have more to say later about the status of my sort of healing in a medical context. For the moment I will just stress that I advise everyone to seek proper medical attention, just as I do myself. My work in no way conflicts with that of medical practitioners; it is complementary.

Of course many people come to me and to other healers only as a last resort, when the medical profession can apparently do no more for them, or so they believe. The profession on the whole nowadays is very much more aware of the possible benefits of the sort of healing I do. I had a little operation recently and I was in the very capable hands of a marvellous surgeon who believes in my work. 'Doris,' he said, 'you come into the hospital and I'll heal you and you'll heal me.'

The tape-recordings of my month-long tour in April and May 1985 are not of particular interest where healing is concerned because the pattern was always the same, but they are quite fascinating when it comes to clairvoyance, where the pattern is similar but every encounter, if I may use that word, is different. It is the clairvoyant experience therefore that I want to concentrate on, although by no means exclusively, in this book.

I know that tapes have often been wiped, or appear to have been wiped, when attempts have been made to record private clairvoyant sessions, or what some people – but not I – choose to call seances. As far as my public sessions are concerned, I have tapes of all but three of the twenty-six engagements to which I have referred. For some reason the tapes are blank which cover my visits to Aberdeen, Ipswich and Scarborough. I have no particular explanation for this. Perhaps someone just forgot to turn the machine on. The tape of my Doncaster meeting also turned out to be of insufficiently good quality.

Before I deal with the tapes as a whole, it may be of interest to tell you what happened at one actual meeting in some detail, and I may as well start with the very first in point of time – at the Brighton Dome – although nothing exceptionally dramatic occurred. It will, however, give the flavour of the sort of thing that takes place, so that readers who have not been to one of my meetings will get some idea of what goes on. When I say that nothing really dramatic occurred that night, I am speaking of course in comparative terms, because I am quite sure that each message was very dramatic indeed to the person or persons in the audience to whom it was addressed.

I never know when the messages will start to come through, although they always do. I have to warm up first, which is why the audience always gets a little chatter from me, until inevitably I make contact with the spirit world.

I have been very interested to listen to the tape of my Brighton meeting because I have no memory of what I may have said. As soon as a meeting is over, what happened is usually right out of my mind, and only something like a newspaper report, or in this case a tape-recording, can tell me what happened. It may be of interest therefore if I start off with a fairly full report of the very first message at Brighton. Although not a very fateful message in this case, it will demonstrate the difficulty I have in interpreting quickly what is said to me and how sometimes I have to fight to get the recipient to understand what I am being told.

If I have all the time in the world, I can try to ask questions myself and get a clearer message. What comes through to me is not always absolutely certain. The trouble with appearing on stage is that I do not have the luxury of being able to take my time. I have to be quick. When I am working I must not dry up. This can create difficulties for me but I am usually able to make some sort of sense of things in the end.

When I say that I am giving a performance, I do not of course mean that I am putting on an act. According to a newspaper report, the magician Paul Daniels is supposed to have offered £10,000 to either Doris Stokes or me if either one of us could convince him that our clairvoyance is genuine by giving a sitting in his home to a person of his choice. The implication must be that he does not believe we are genuine, if of course he was correctly reported, which I doubt. I am not qualified to examine the work of magicians and I am sure that Mr Daniels cannot be qualified to examine the work of clairvoyants. In fact I am sure that he must be very ignorant about my work. I have been tested by serious scientists, but I am not a freak in a circus side-show and my work is in no way connected with magical tricks. I do not need to be tested by a magician, whose approval in any case I have never sought. I am far too old for party tricks and if Mr Daniels has £10,000 to spare, I can suggest any number of worthy charities that would be delighted to hear from him.

If he is under the mistaken impression that all clairvoyants are really only magicians, I wish he would attend one of my public meetings. They are open to anyone who buys a ticket. I wonder what he would have thought had he watched me over a period of a month, working in a different way every night; or what indeed he would have made of my very first message in Brighton, let alone the more sensational messages to which I shall refer later.

At Brighton I first went to a gentleman sitting right in front of me. 'The gentleman in a grey suit,' I said. There was a lady sitting next to him whom he confirmed was his wife. 'I have your father,' I told him. 'He said immediately to me, "I want to go to my boy." '

I had hardly hesitated before going directly to this man, so I am sure his father must have guided me to him very positively. Sometimes I have to go to more than one person before I find the right one for whom a message is intended.

'Your father was very interested while I was talking,' I told his son in the audience. 'Now who is John, because he says he has met John?'

The man indicated that he knew who was meant. (Of course John is a very common name and I suppose most people know a John, but I cannot help that. Sometimes I am given much more unusual, even foreign, names.)

'Now your father's also given me a condition of the lady's back. Perhaps the lady next to you, your wife.'

'No.'

'Well, he went right to the bottom of the back. Is it yours then?'

'Mine, yes.'

'Now you have got healing ability.'

'So they tell me.'

'What have you done about it?'

'I'm learning.'

'There's only one way to learn and that's to get on with the job.'

'That's what people keep telling me.'

'You have given your wife healing.'

'Yes.'

'Didn't you go to the top of her neck?'

'I did, yes.'

'Thank you. Now I'm going to explain exactly what I mean. She had some problem with her back. Didn't she fall off three steps?'

The lady spoke for the first time. 'No, it's not me who had the bad back,' she said, 'it's my husband.'

'I know he has a bad back. Forget him for the moment. Didn't you have some problem, perhaps some time ago? You see, I'm getting a condition and I think his father is talking about you. Didn't you fall off some steps?'

'No.'

'Well, it must be you, sir.' I had obviously misunderstood his father.

'I fell about ten years ago,' his son agreed.

'Off some steps?'

'Yes.'

I had perhaps not made a very good start. 'It's a funny thing,' I continued, 'because all the time I'm here with you, someone is playing a violin.'

'That I can't work out at the moment.'

'I'll have to take you back. I'm going to take you back to when you were a boy. Can you go back to where you lived? I'm seeing a row of houses, about six or seven in a row. You lived in one of those with your mother and your father.'

'That's right.'

'He's showing the house to me, and two doors away there was somebody there who would play music or a violin. I hear it going on all the time.'

'Yes, there was a violin played in that home.'

'Now the person who played the violin is here too.'

'I see.'

'Do you understand that?'

'Yes.'

'One, two, three,' I suddenly changed the subject. 'Are you one of three children?'

'Yes.'

'Because he said to me, "One, two, three." And who is Harry?'

'I can't place Harry.'

'You should because you work or worked with him. At one time in your life, he said, you were together. Don't think of your family.'

'I've worked with so many people, I can't place him.'

I was unable to pursue this matter because the father suddenly brought a lady to me. 'He has brought your mother. No, I think it is the mother of the lady. Do you understand this?'

It was she who answered, 'Yes.'

'I rather think both your mothers are here, but I am definitely getting the mother who wants to talk to her daughter. Do you know Elizabeth? Because she says, "Will you tell my daughter I have met Elizabeth?" and you may have to think about that because it may be someone just outside the family link. She says you're like your father.'

'Maybe, yes, but I think I'm more like my mother.'

'She says to me you're more like your father because you've got your father's nose, and although in many ways you look like your mother, you have a lot of – oh, I've suddenly got your father now. Excuse me, I've got to be careful what I say or I shall get the whole family. He's saying, "Nelly." '

'Yes.'

'Who's that?'

'An aunt.'

'Closely linked with your mother?'

'Yes.'

'Because she said – this is your mother again – "Tell her Nelly is here, and she resembles Nelly more than she resembles me, and she has got her father's nose." I don't know why they're going into this detail. Now, you had some problem just before you came in about changing some money.'

'Did I?'

'Your husband did.'

'No.'

'Yes,' I insisted.

'I won't agree with you.'

'That's all right. I can only tell you that your father just said to me that there was a transference of money.'

'I can't think what it was,' the man now said.

'I've got to tell you, have I? A bit of detail – who has asked you for money?'

'I can't think of anybody.'

'Oddly enough, I'm right away from Brighton altogether. Wait a minute. He's showing me a will. Do you understand this? A will.'

'No, I can't understand.'

'Before you say no, there must have been some problem over a will. Quite definitely. He tells me you've made your will.'

'Yes, that's correct.'

'And there was some problem with what you wanted to do.'

'My will was made many, many years ago.'

'I realise that but things have changed and you've moved.'

'That's right.'

'And there was a discussion about the transfer – I keep seeing money. My goodness me, I didn't know you were rich!'

'Neither did I,' was the reply, provoking laughter from the audience who must have felt that I was having a difficult time with this couple.

'Your father is still showing me money, a transference of some sort. Some sort of change. Perhaps if you talk to your wife, she'll understand a bit better than you.'

'Oh, we have been talking over some transfers of property.'

The audience started to clap very heartily.

'Thank you,' I said. 'I told you I had to be careful because he said to me, "Now don't tell everybody everything." Do you understand now?'

'Yes, thank you.'

'I tried to keep it as private as I could. Your father is insisting that you get rid of – have you three properties?'

'No.'

'He again said to me, "One, two, three." '

'I only have one property. No, I have two properties actually.'

'But were you thinking of getting something else?'

'We are thinking of another place.'

'Well, that's three properties.'

'We haven't got it yet.'

'You will.'

'Thank you.'

'Because your father spoke about three properties. He said you should be very careful and think very carefully about what you are going to do with the other property. Do you understand?'

'Yes.'

'He said – oh, goodness me, he's giving me a load of information here – you've already discussed what you'd like to do with it.'

'Correct.'

'But he said, "Be careful." And I'm going to tell you something else he said: "We are given our relations, thank God we can choose our friends." '

I have related the above experience almost verbatim, not just because it happened to be the first message of my first meeting on my month's tour but also because it is typical of many messages I received that are unremarkable in content. It would have been very easy to have begun with an example in which I had come up with a clear, direct and dramatic message but I deliberately wanted to start with something unremarkable in content and even confusing. The message may mean very little to anybody else but I hope it was important to the people who received it. At least I hope it confirmed to them that they were genuinely in touch with their loved ones in the spirit world.

What is not always realised is that however urgently someone who has passed over may wish to communicate with someone on the earth plane, he or she may talk about events that happened a long time ago, events which younger people may not readily remember.

The reader is welcome to pick my first message to pieces, to say that I am wrong most of the time, that I am making generalities that apply to almost anyone, and so on. Everyone knows someone called John; everyone has a bad back; everyone looks like their parents; everyone changes money – it is easy to make this sort of charge. Later on, I shall give many examples of a more extraordinary nature, where it is more difficult to sustain this sort of criticism, but I want the reader to realise that I am human and not some sort of infallible computer. I am not interested in making claims for myself beyond saying that I have the gift to contact the spirit world.

I do not invent messages. I am merely a medium through whom messages are relayed. I do no more than pass on what I learn. Later I will explain how I function as a psychic, but in fact I am like a postman delivering a letter, except that the letter comes from another plane and is often almost illegible.

If someone from the spirit world mentions the name Harry to me, I pass it on; perhaps I have misheard it, misunderstood it or misinterpreted it. If the recipient does not understand it, that does not mean that it is necessarily wrong. Indeed, I have to believe what I am told, and usually its truth becomes apparent, if not always instantly.

Many of the people who receive these communications derive great comfort from the possibility, or in some cases the certainty, that there is survival after death and that they can be in touch with their loved ones who have passed over. It would be the most dreadful and heartless pursuit on my part to foster such belief if I did not share it. I may not entirely understand my gift, but I know beyond doubt that it is genuine, and there are thousands, if not millions, of people who know this. In the face of their support, I can ignore uninformed critics.

I wish that Paul Daniels had been present at Brighton. He would have had the opportunity to gather considerable further evidence. My second message was directed to a lady at the back of the theatre. It was from a young man who had died following an accident. I felt some sort of impact and he was showing me wheels, so I realised that he had been hit while driving a car or riding a motorbike. He told me that he had been rushed to hospital but had lived only a very short time.

A lady at the back of the audience identified herself. She had known this young man, and I was convinced that the message was for her. The young man asked me to tell her that he had loved her and said that he was terribly sorry that he had left her alone.

He kept showing me two rings and his photograph in a brown folder, but at first this meant nothing to the lady until she remembered that she had the young man's photograph in an album. He asked me to tell her that he was not at fault and wondered why she was afraid to talk to him. 'She used to talk to me for hours,' he said.

He told me that she had reshaped her life, which she confirmed. 'Tell her not to be afraid,' he continued, 'I am no different.' Then he wished her all the luck in the world but added: 'Don't forget me. Once I was most important to you.' Then he took me up some steps to a third-floor flat where they had been together and where he had given her a ring, the significance of which the lady now realised.

My third message that night was rather strange, and I shall not attempt to interpret it. I was directed to a whole row of men at the back of the balcony, and I felt what I described as 'a great deal of lack of communication'. There were at least six of them who were there for a specific purpose. 'You won't get it,' I told their spokesman, 'but remember that God heals, not the Devil. That's your answer.'

The man said he did not understand, to which I replied: 'You jolly well do, the whole lot of you. I'm psychic and I can see your whole aura and you are speaking as one person.'

Message number four was directed at a lady in a bright red dress in the second row. It was from a man who had died as a result of a breathing problem. He told me that he knew he would die and that he positively hated the hospital to which he had been taken. He said that he had met the lady's mother in the spirit world.

Then the lady's father came through to me. He mentioned the name Lily, which the lady said was the name of her cousin, and also Ted, which in fact was her father's name. She could not make sense, however, of his references to Florrie or Flo and to two boys whom he indicated she had known in her childhood. He said that he was a man of few words, but when he did speak, everyone was fully aware of it.

He then started showing me a bottle of tablets, and I asked the lady what was wrong with her medically. She said there was nothing wrong with her, except for her nerves, but there was great hilarity in the audience as I was able to diagnose that she had trouble in walking and that she had taken tablets for rheumatism in her feet! I ended by offering to give her healing on stage later that evening.

A woman from the spirit world came to me next and asked for her daughter. I received the name Williamson and asked if there was anyone of that name in the theatre. A lady raised her hand but I did not feel that she was in the right part of the audience, and I doubted if the communication was for her. I eventually identified the right person, whose father's name was Williams. 'That's my daughter, she's got my ring,' the spirit confirmed, and asked me to thank the daughter for all she had done for her and to let her know that she had remained cheerful until the end.

She then spoke of Dorothy, who turned out to be her daughter-in-law and who she described as a chatterbox. Next she asked for Harry, who was in fact her son-in-law and sitting with his wife. 'Why doesn't Harry speak up?' she asked.

She then had the audience in stitches as she spoke about false teeth. She told me that she only put her teeth in to eat, and that Harry now had a similar problem.

'Yes,' Harry confirmed, 'but it's the other way round. I take them out when I eat.' He also said that when he was not wearing them, he kept them in a bag.

My contact then spoke about Harry's father, who was still on the earth plane. She told Harry that his father was fitter than he was, much to Harry's amusement. Then she returned to her daughter, saying that the daughter regularly ticked off the days on a calendar. 'I don't know why she does it,' she said impishly, 'because she doesn't do anything with the days.'

Suddenly the woman was showing me a shed. 'You've got a shed,' I said. 'No,' said the daughter. 'Well, she's walked me down a garden path,' I insisted, 'and you had a shed.' 'Oh yes,' came the reply, 'where I used to live.'

'Where you used to live, you had a shed and when your husband got annoyed, he'd go into the shed. But he never did anything in the shed,' I added.

'Your mother is very amusing,' I said, and the audience was laughing heartily at her sense of humour. 'And why shouldn't I be?' she told me. 'I'm just the same now as I always was.'

I was next directed to a woman in the audience by a man who said that he had gassed himself. He said that he had made a previous attempt at suicide and apologised for the trouble he had caused, but asked the lady to understand that there was no other way out for him. He spoke of two children and I rather felt that they were not related to him, but I must have been wrong because the lady said she had two children whom the man had never seen in his life.

He kept speaking of twenty-two, or two and two, which made no sense to the lady, and I had great difficulty in trying to make sense of it myself, for forces were trying to pull me away from the man, as I told the audience. I eventually decided that the man must have helped her son over some difficulty when the boy was twenty-two.

There is of course always a certain tension in the air when suicides come through. It is a different sort of tension from that created by someone who has died a natural death, such as my next contact, a woman who had died from cancer, who went to her daughter in the front row. The girl said that she had come along hoping to hear from her mother.

The woman put two rings in my hand, which enabled me to tell the girl that she already had an engagement ring but that she had her eyes on a wedding ring. 'Does he know how much it's going to cost?' I asked.

'I haven't told him yet,' the girl answered, indicating her fiancé at her side.

'Oh dear,' I said, 'this is a bit dodgy. Your mother says there was somebody else.'

'That's right,' the girl agreed.

'But that would have been a big mistake. You let the other one go very quickly. "Should I run after him and get him back?" you thought. But you didn't run very far. Your mother wishes you and your new fiancé all the best in the world.'

I was then distracted by the sound of a banjo playing, but the girl was unable to help me to interpret the significance of the music. I went back to her mother, who told me her daughter's young man was not yet ready to get married and settle down. I turned my attention to him, and he agreed that they had not yet set a date for the marriage but that the girl was pushing him.

Her mother then told me that the young man was sick of working for other people and that he was not very good with his boss. 'You want something of your own,' I said, 'where the two of you can work together.'

He agreed. 'But that's got nothing to do with getting married,' I said. 'You're looking for a double job. What you're after is a licence – over the door!'

I think his next words were 'Bloody hell!' and when he had recovered from his surprise, 'Yes,' he said, 'that's what we're after, a pub.'

'Mother says, remember not to drink the profits,' I went on. 'It's better if you're married. You stand a better chance.'

Then I passed on another message from the girl's mother: 'You're going to get what you want next year, she said, so you ought to get married this year. She wants to see you happily settled. Remember your dad, she said, she doesn't want to see history repeat itself.'

It would be interesting of course to know what has happened to this young couple, whether in fact they got married and got their pub, and whether they are happy together. But of course had I not been able to hear the tape, I would have remembered nothing about this.

My message about the licence over the door seemed to attract loud applause, and I must have looked up to where the young men had been sitting to whom I had given the third message of the night. Perhaps they had come with the intention of disrupting proceedings, or as a negative influence. As I now announced to the whole audience, they had all disappeared.

The eighth message was from a man who had drowned. I had a feeling of water coming over me and I saw a man in a uniform, but I did not think he was a sailor although he told me that his ship had gone down with all hands during the last war. He was wearing something white, so I wondered if he had been a steward in the Merchant Navy.

A young girl at the back thought this might be her grandfather whom she had never met, but I did not feel that the man was trying to contact her. It was someone else in the same area, and eventually I found a woman whose father had been in the Army and who had drowned when his troopship was bombed. That would explain the uniform and why I had been convinced he was not a sailor; I was not sure about the significance of whatever he was wearing that was white, but the woman suggested that it might have been a lifebelt.

He spoke to me of Will or Bill, and Bill turned out to be his best friend – and the lady's mother's best friend too. The last thing he had told his wife before going overseas was, 'If anything happens to me, don't marry Bill,' although he admitted that Bill was a jolly good chap and had helped his widow to get over his death at sea.

I then felt a terrific pressure on my head, and I asked the lady in the audience whether she suffered from headaches. No, she said, but her mother had suffered from migraine. At that very moment her mother came to me also. She was bouncing with excitement, quite a contrast to her husband. 'She's just like a bubble,' I said.

She told me how much her daughter looked like her and described a family holiday in Torquay. Then she had a message for her daughter. She told me that there had been a change in the daughter's life. 'Hip hip hooray!' she said, and gave her certain personal advice that is not perhaps worth repeating here because it could only make sense to the lady concerned.

I was next directed to the balcony where a party of four people were seated. Three of them had come together and had met up with the fourth outside, but the man who came to me from the spirit world seemed to belong to two of them in particular, a man and a woman. They turned out to be brother and sister, and the man was their grandfather.

I kept doing something with my hands. 'What sort of manual work do you do?' I asked the brother. 'I'm in the carpet business,' he said. 'No, it's not that,' I insisted. 'Could it be writing?' the brother asked. But I knew that my hands were not operating like a writer's.

'It must be your grandfather, then,' I said. 'He must have worked with his hands.'

'No,' said the brother.

'Yes,' I said. 'Yes, quite definitely.'

'Could it be gardening?' the sister asked. 'Grandfather was a gardener.'

'No,' I said, 'he's not showing me that sort of movement. He wasn't a bellringer, was he? I feel I keep pulling something, and somebody's going up and down. What was it?'

'It was a rope,' the sister suddenly realised. 'He was a lift operator, but he did it by hand. He was a manual lift operator.'

'That's it,' I said, as I immediately recognised what my hands had been doing.

The grandfather then introduced a woman called Rose, whom the brother and sister said was an aunt who had just passed over. She was nervous and was instructed to speak up by the grandfather. 'Do you think I dare?' she asked.

The man then showed me someone who was a stonemason and undertaker, and the sister confirmed that his father had been a stonemason. He then told her that she had psychic gifts, like her grandmother; and told her brother that he had healing gifts.

The tenth and last message that night in Brighton was very brief. It was a message of comfort for a woman in the audience from a very elderly lady who had died suddenly. 'You've been having such a lot of problems, but there's nothing to worry about. Don't keep looking back, stop worrying and don't be afraid.'

This was all in an evening's work – followed as usual by a healing session.

CHAPTER 3

The Evidence of the Tapes

I have already described what happened at the first of my meetings during my month-long tour of the country in April and May 1985. I have since had the fascinating experience of listening to tapes of twenty of the other twenty-four meetings.

It appears that I went to an average of eight people each night, and there are actually 162 case histories on record. Thirty-nine concerned people who had passed over as a result of illness, almost half of them from heart attacks or some heart condition. Twenty-five people had died following an accident. As many as sixteen had committed suicide, four had been killed in the war and three had been murdered. The rest died of natural causes.

Looked at in one way, this is a pretty grim catalogue, and it may be that people who have died in violent or mysterious circumstances sometimes have greater motivation to contact their loved ones to try to bring them comfort. It is a highly emotional experience for someone to receive a message from a person who has passed over in some distress, but it is surprising how often humour manifests itself on these occasions and how laughter and tears seem to go hand in hand together. I have been told that my meetings are never depressing, and I can hear from the tapes how very funny my conversations often are.

Some critics have complained that I introduce levity into deadly serious matters. If a person has hanged himself and nevertheless makes a joke, why should I not report what he has told me? In any case I mean no disrespect and I do not believe that people who are receiving messages from the other side which they believe to be genuine will object to other people, in other words the audience around them, intruding temporarily into their private world. It can help to have others share your sorrows and laugh with you – never at you. That is the point.

It would be tedious to describe all these tapes in detail, but I want to pick out some of the more interesting examples, not only from this particular tour but also from the earlier tour I made two months before, which was widely reported in the local Press.

To emphasise the often humorous nature of the communications, let me start off with some examples of messages that those who heard them thought were very funny. In Worthing, for example, a regimental sergeant major on the other side asked to speak to his wife in the audience. He told me that he had been a difficult man to live with because he liked to run his home like an Army camp. He kept telling his wife to stand up straight, and she had the audience in stitches when she told me that death had obviously not changed her husband at all.

At the Edinburgh Playhouse another man came to his widow. He told me that she had not been with him at the end. 'I was alone when I died,' he said, 'but I'm glad. We said goodbye, and I knew I wouldn't see her again in this life.' Then he told me that she had some problem with her ear. 'Did you have attention?' I asked.

'I went to see about a deaf aid,' she replied, 'but I won't use it. It's in the house in the drawer.'

Then the husband said something quite funny to me. 'All that money wasted,' were his words, 'not only on her ears but on her teeth too.'

When I reported this comment, for some reason there were peals of laughter in the Playhouse, which may have disconcerted the lady because she said, 'That's nonsense.'

The husband then told me that he knew his wife very well. 'He is glad to have made everybody laugh,' I told her. 'He was a happy man and if he could crack a joke, he would. Are you happy now?' I asked.

I realised that I may have misheard his earlier remark

about his wife's teeth, for he was now telling me that there was something wrong with her *feet*, but she denied this too.

'No,' I was able to say, 'he said it's not your feet, it's your shoes.' For some reason the audience went into almost hysterical laughter.

'Your husband is a real comedian,' I told the lady. 'He said you've got to have a hat not just for Sunday but for every day of the week.'

Then he returned to the subject of his wife's ear. It was the left one that gave her problems, and he insisted that she put the deaf aid in the correct place and not leave it in a drawer.

'I will,' the lady said. 'I am going to put it in my ear.'

At that point the lady's mother-in-law came to me, and also started talking about her daughter-in-law's health. 'She says if you keep your chest warm, you'll be all right,' I said.

'They're a funny lot, this family,' I had to comment. They certainly had the audience amused, and I hope that the lady realised that the laughter was sympathetic and that people were laughing with her and not, as I said before, at her.

A message at Chatham had its funny side too. A man who had been dead about ten years asked for his son and took us back eight years to an emotional time in the son's life.

'Did you move at that time?' I asked.

'No.'

I insisted, because the father was certain.

'Oh yes,' the son said, 'we moved next door.'

The father then gave me the impression of piling a lot of cars in front of me. 'What do you do for a living?' I asked the son.

He said he was a bus driver. 'But you haven't always done that. Your father says you've had four separate different sorts of work.' The son agreed.

'He says you've had a precarious life. You've had to battle your way.'

The father then wrote a number. It was probably either 146 or 148. 'Is that a bus you drive?' I asked.

'Sometimes,' the son agreed.

'Your father has a dry sense of humour – and so do you,' I continued. 'Have you had some problem with one ear?'

'Two ears,' was the reply. 'I'm partly deaf.'

'Do the bus company know?'

'We keep that quiet.'

'All right,' I said quickly, 'I won't say anything, but your father says you're supposed to hear as well as see.'

The audience seemed to find this quite funny.

'What did your father do?' I asked.

'He was a plumber.'

'Did he train you as a plumber?'

'No, that was my brother.'

'But your brother didn't make it.'

'No, he wasn't that interested.'

'Did your brother do some plumbing in your house?' I enquired.

'I hope not,' was the emphatic reply, at which the audience again fell about.

'Your father says everything your brother touched broke into pieces. He says whatever you do, don't let him near the water tubes.' There was more laughter.

But the bus driver's father was not finished. He seemed very concerned with his son's domestic arrangements.

'What's wrong with your kitchen?' I asked.

'I want to expand it.'

'Well, don't,' I said. 'Your father says you never finish what you're doing, and whatever you do, don't let your brother near it. You'd be better off selling up and moving somewhere where the kitchen's already done. Your wife wants a kitchen – not a gaping hole in the wall.'

You can imagine how this amused the audience and, I

hope, the bus driver, whose father had already told me that his son was unhappy in Chatham and had been thinking about moving for two years. He ended up by telling his son that if he waited, he would find what he wanted. He would definitely make a change.

His last words to me were: 'I never thought I'd come back and manage this, but I did manage it!'

There was laughter in the audience at Margate too when a number of people from the spirit world came to a woman in the audience.

The woman's mother told me that her daughter had changed her mind three times about her current gentleman friend. 'He's no good for you,' was her message, 'but you won't listen.'

As if to reinforce matters, the woman's grandmother intervened. 'You're made for far better things,' she told her granddaughter. 'You don't want a cart to push. You want to sit in it and be drawn. You want somebody to make decisions for you, but you'll never get that, dear. If I were you, I'd look around a bit.'

The grandmother then had the audience in stitches as she advised: 'Spread your wings. That's just what your mother did. I had a lot of trouble with your mother.'

She then told me that the mother had been very fond of aspidistras, which she used to polish with milk.

There was no shortage of people with messages for this particular lady. A man came to me who described the house where she lived when she was much younger, and mentioned a nearby alley.

'I've got someone from the spirit world who was up an alley with you,' I told her, which seemed to amuse the audience enormously.

'He says he loved you very much but you always ran away.'

'Just as well I did,' was the lady's reply.

I am always pleased when there is laughter in the air. Shakespeare knew that he had to introduce comic relief in the midst of tragedy, which might otherwise be too much to bear. Joy and sadness often walk hand in hand, and tears and laughter both play their part in life.

I will come to the tragedies shortly, the people who were murdered or committed suicide, those who died in war and in accidents, who came through with messages for the loved ones they had left behind; and of course the people who died following illness – but even they could sometimes be amusing. I often wonder whether the dead do not have a better sense of humour than the living.

Let me first, however, refer to one or two messages that had a slightly unusual quality. At my meeting in Edinburgh, a father came to his daughter in the audience. He told me about his wife who had a lot of trouble before she died. She always had difficulties and, through him, she wanted to thank her daughter for all her understanding.

'I can't imagine her saying that,' the daughter responded, obviously surprised and perhaps disbelieving.

'Well,' I insisted, 'that's what she's saying now. She wants to come back to give you her love – and will you accept it? She says you shouldn't hold the bitterness because it harms you.'

'I try every day,' the daughter said.

'Let it go,' I continued, passing on the mother's message which I was getting through the father. '"A great deal wasn't my fault," she says, "it was the circumstances of my life." She wants your husband to know that she misunderstood the whole situation. It's as if she turned her back on him and walked away. Will he please forgive her? She says she couldn't show her inner thoughts to him.'

I then asked the daughter if she had put her father on a

pedestal. She agreed that this was so. 'I have a feeling,' I said, 'that your mother was jealous.'

'She was,' the daughter said.

'You thought everything your father did was right and what she did wasn't.'

'Correct.'

'She says that you can't be that bitter because you still have her photograph. As a child, you thought you were the odd one out. You wouldn't go towards her, you wouldn't open and share your heart with her, and she was too stern.'

'That's very true.'

'"If you can forgive me," she says, "it will give me peace."'

I told the daughter that her parents were now together. 'Your mother says you never thought that would happen. They were like oil and water, but he no longer bears a grudge.'

Then the mother, still through the medium of the father, explained what her daughter obviously thought was her mother's bad behaviour. '"It was because I grew up," she said, "with no love. I had a mother and father who showed no affection."'

Then I said to the daughter, 'You had a brother, but with him it was different. He came forward and was made your mother's favourite. He told you, "Don't be like mother." Do you understand that?'

'Yes, I do,' the daughter replied sadly, 'that's my dread.'

'Put your arms around your husband,' I told her, 'and tell him how much you love him. Don't shut him out. That is your mother's message, and she says if she can get that through to you, then she's achieved something.'

It is interesting that it was the father who manifested himself to me but the mother who really wanted to communicate.

Another interesting communication occurred at a big meeting at the Dominion Theatre in London. I went to a man right at the front in one of the best seats. 'I have your mother here,' I told him. 'She's come with a lot of music.'

'She played piano,' he said.

Whether or not I detected an American accent, I cannot say, but I asked him why his mother was taking me across the Atlantic.

'I was born in Philadelphia,' he said.

'Your mother has a very definite personality, and you have the same. Have you got a moustache?'

I should perhaps explain that I cannot always see the people in the audiences to whom I am directed. The lighting systems are designed for the audiences to see me, and not the other way round.

Apparently the man did have a moustache. 'You've had it off twice,' I said, 'your mother's just told me. Now she's showing me a lot of horses.'

'I had a bad horseback riding accident,' the man said.

'You cracked your leg, and it affected your hip and your back,' I went on, 'and you're still in pain. What have you done about it?'

'Not a lot,' he said.

'Are you satisfied to have this?' I asked. 'You should do something about it.'

Then I asked another question: 'Have you just bought some property? Your mother says you weren't sure about it. Would you be surprised if you had some more? You've got some money to invest and you don't know what to do about it.'

'Probably,' he said.

'I know what to do about it,' I said, ever alive apparently to the main chance even when communicating with the spirit world, 'I want a healing centre – but you're not ready for that yet.'

Then the man's father came to me. 'He says you're the same as him on top,' I told the man, 'and to tell you that grass doesn't grow on busy streets. You didn't get off to a very good start, but he's proud of what you've achieved. You've had an emotional break in your life. "Tell him," he says, "life isn't as big a problem as he thinks. Life isn't over. There will be more peace and contentment than you realise."'

I suppose it is noteworthy how many people from the spirit world claim to see into our future.

'You have three children,' I said.

'Yes,' the man agreed.

'Your father says you live in two places at once.'

'I just built a new house,' the man replied.

'You're going to have another desk.'

'That's true.'

'Would you be surprised if you built a third house?'

'I most certainly would.'

'Well, you will, you'll see.'

What I did not know was that the man in question was a great friend of my manager. He was on a visit to London with his wife and they were present in the theatre as my manager's guests. Had I been aware of this, as I have already explained, I doubt if I would have gone to the gentleman with a message, although of course I am not sure to what extent I have any control over where I am directed.

I have to ask the reader to believe that I had never met the man or even heard of him before that evening, but he and his wife were among the guests at a late dinner, following the 'performance', given jointly by my manager and the promoter.

It was at this dinner that I was given the golden disc by the promoter, not unlike those given to pop stars when they sell a million copies of a record. It is inscribed with the words: 'To Doris Collins, in recognition of her record-breaking on-the-road meetings'.

The man to whom I had passed on messages from his parents turned out to be a film producer from California who acted as business manager to a number of very well-known people in the entertainment industry. He told me at the dinner that I had been remarkably accurate in what I had told him.

He said that while I was talking to him from the stage of the theatre, he had a curious feeling of being connected with me, as if by a thin thread. He could not describe it more exactly, but it was as if there were a piece of cotton joining us together. Although many people write to me, or talk to me briefly after a meeting, it is extremely rare to meet somebody socially to whom I have been a medium for the communication of messages from the spirit world, and his comment about some sort of physical conduit between us struck me as interesting.

At my meeting in Ayr, I was directed to a woman sitting in the balcony by a man from the spirit world. I was given the surname Maxwell, and it turned out that the man was her father. He told me that she had had to struggle to achieve what she wanted in life and that she often felt that she was swimming against the tide with other people wanting to interfere, although she knew exactly what she wanted.

'Do you draw?' I asked, explaining that her father seemed to be trying to sketch something.

'Yes,' she said.

But not for a living, I felt. 'What do you do as work?' I asked.

'I'm a lecturer,' she said.

'Your father is telling me that you had to change your profession and didn't think it was going to be successful.'

'Quite right,' she agreed.

'Why is it you want to go abroad? You were thinking of going abroad but he says, "Don't do it yet."'

He said something to me about February and March, but I could not interpret it and it seemed to mean nothing to his daughter. 'When you say you're a lecturer, what do you lecture in?' I asked.

'Catering,' was the reply.

This was obviously not what I expected to hear because the father was still apparently sketching. 'Apart from drawing,' I asked, suddenly understanding, 'don't you paint?'

The woman agreed that she did.

'That's where your heart is,' I told her. 'Your father says this is what you should have done because you're very talented. But you felt you couldn't have gotten anywhere.'

'I wonder sometimes,' the woman said.

Then I told her that her father was putting two wedding rings on my finger, one of which he blew away as if to indicate that a particular marriage had not lasted and was no good.

'You've not been married twice?' I asked, rather uncertainly.

'Yes,' she agreed.

'Don't do it, he says, the timing is wrong and you'll make another mistake. You want your freedom, but he says you won't have freedom if you do it that way. He says do it only when it's all wrapped up – financially.' He stressed the last word.

'Don't open the door and walk out,' I told her.

Also at Ayr I had a curious double message for two ladies sitting together. Or to be more precise there were two separate messages from different people in the spirit world who were unconnected. I knew that these ladies were unrelated but it was clear to me that they did a great deal together. Although the greatest of friends, they were almost like twins.

The first lady had a communication from a very determined woman.

'Have you just moved?' I enquired.

'Yes,' the lady said.

'Packing and getting things together has worn you out,' I told her.

'That's right,' she agreed.

'She says you are like her, and everything has to be in the right place.'

'Exactly,' the lady confirmed.

'You don't do as much cooking as you used to.'

'No.'

'Now it's a quick job on toast,' I said. 'She taught you to be such a good cook but now you don't bother. She says there is no nourishment in that. It's your mother, of course. "There's no nourishment in that," she keeps repeating.'

Then a man came into my view. His name was Bill.

'Bill has come,' I said, 'who's that?'

'That's my Dad.'

'And who's John?' I enquired.

'His brother, my uncle. You'll be in a right old mess,' the lady added, 'he had a lot of brothers.'

'Your father keeps jingling money in front of me,' I went on. 'Was he a bit careful with cash?'

'He didn't have a lot, but he was careful with what he had,' the lady agreed.

'He said, "Look after the pennies and the shillings will take care of themselves." He said, "We had to stretch it like a piece of elastic." But you've had an education, and you made best use of what you had.'

Suddenly the father started telling me about the Prince of

Wales. I did not think he was referring to the heir to the throne. 'It must be a pub,' I said. 'Do you understand that?'

'I knew the Prince of Wales,' was the lady's enigmatic reply, 'but I did not know that he frequented it actually.'

'Someone connected with your father worked there,' I said. 'Hold on, he's put some uniform on. That was when he was associated with the Prince of Wales. Now you'll know what I'm talking about.'

'He was a dedicated soldier,' the lady said.

'Of course, he was in Army uniform. I wasn't sure but he just saluted me like that. He was a great one for clean shoes and regimentation, and you were brought up like that.'

The lady agreed.

All the while the other spirit was waiting, as it were, in the aisles, to speak to the lady's friend. Turning to the companion at her side, I told her that a man was there who had passed very quickly. He wanted to tell her how sorry he was that he had to go so suddenly, but he was delighted that she had managed to stand on her own feet.

Then he said something very strange. 'Sometimes you smell tobacco in the house,' I told her.

'Yes,' she admitted.

'Well, he says that where you smell it, that's where he is.'

CHAPTER 4

Always Extraordinary

Before I deal with suicide and murder, I want to refer to some less sensational instances, and I have selected some cases of people who passed in accidents and others who passed after some form of illness.

Sometimes I have picked on an example deliberately because it is ordinary. A message of help and comfort from the spirit world can often be something very simple. It is no less a bond of love between this earth plane and the next because it is undramatic. In fact the very ordinariness of communication is often the best evidence of survival after death.

However ordinary a message may seem, please remember that to the person to whom it is directed it is always extraordinary.

I went to a man in Preston with a message from a small child who had died of meningitis. 'I can't see the child,' I said, 'I can only feel it.'

The man was the child's father. 'She was two weeks old,' he said.

'Do you have two other children?' I asked.

'Yes,' he said.

'This death was very traumatic for you.'

'It broke my heart,' he confessed.

'Now a man has come in. It's your grandfather. He says don't break your heart because the child was an old soul and only came for a short time. She brought a blessing that nothing else could have done. You have a grandchild?'

'One, a boy.'

'Your grandson is the blessing your own little child has left behind,' was the message.

At my meeting in Sheffield I went to a married couple in the first row. I had a message from the man's father and I felt a pressure on my chest, so I asked whether he had died of a heart condition. This proved correct.

Then the woman's father shot into my consciousness. The two fathers were together, probably as they had never been in their lives on earth. As if this was not enough, the woman's mother also appeared, followed by a man whose relationship with the couple was at first unclear.

'I have a man from Poland,' I said. 'Do you understand that?'

Neither husband nor wife could make sense of this. 'Are you sure?' I said. 'He's certainly from Europe, from Poland, I think, or perhaps from Germany.'

'I used to work with someone who was a Pole,' the husband suddenly said.

'That's the man,' I stated, 'he says you used to work together. And you certainly never thought he'd come back to say hullo. He just disappeared and left the scene, but you were a kind friend to him, you stood up for him, you tried to understand him, so he wanted to come back and thank you.'

The wife's mother then gave her a message about her health, and both her mother and father then gave me information about her. 'You have been given the gift so that you can translate messages,' I said. 'You are psychic. Was your husband at first against this?'

'No, never.'

'Well, your mother says it has been difficult for you to be able to do what you want.'

'I can't follow this,' the lady said, 'all the family were for it.'

'You have been promised a certain gift,' I persisted, 'and it hasn't fully materialised. What sort of gift? I think it must be a psychic gift and you have not fully developed it.'

'I gave it up some time ago.'

'There you are,' I said, 'but there is much more work for you to do and timing is important. There is a brick wall but it's not the right time to take it down. Yes, you came up against a brick wall but the time will come when it will go down for you. Finally your mother and father are telling you not to get involved with people. Stand alone.'

That is an example of four different people, three relations and a workmate, seeking all to communicate with the same couple. I can never be sure of the meaning of messages to the people who receive them, but I am sure that all communications have a significance for those to whom they are addressed.

In Birmingham a mother, who had died following a heart attack, came to me with a message for her daughter, who she told me was the youngest of her five children.

'There was a problem with the date of your marriage,' I told the daughter, who agreed that it had been changed. 'I must try to be diplomatic,' I said. 'Who's Ted?'

'That's my husband,' was the answer.

'I thought so, because your mother says she didn't approve of Ted at first, but he has turned out better than she thought. Is he careful with his money?' I asked.

'No, not really,' the daughter replied.

'Well, your mother's showing me money. I wonder why. She says when you want something, you have to look after the pennies.'

The mother must then have put me in mind of hair because I asked her daughter: 'Do you do hair?'

'I did my mother-in-law's the other night,' she said.

'Is she there?' I asked.

'No, but my sister-in-law is.'

'Your mother says she's a nice lady, but never mind about your mother-in-law,' which seemed to amuse the audience.

A man came to me in Leicester who had died of cancer. He had a message for a lady whom I thought was probably his wife. It turned out that he was her first husband. He told me that he was too young to die and spoke about his daughter.

'She's lovely,' he said, 'but I couldn't bring her up.' He then asked his wife to thank her new husband for being a good father to the girl.

'You've moved,' I said.

'Yes,' the lady agreed.

'He says, "You've got a nice place, and you've done better for my daughter than I could have done for her. I've watched my girl grow up. She's a bit of you and a bit of me. She's very stubborn."'

'She is!'

'"That was me," he says. "My death affected her but she's got over it now."'

He ended by paying a lovely tribute to his wife. 'I was difficult,' he said, 'but you were everything to me. You gave me the best years of my life.' And he asked his wife to give his daughter his other ring when she grew up.

In Harlow a man came to me who had passed with a heart condition. I gathered that he had suffered a lot of pain. 'I knew my time was up two years before,' he said, 'but when the end came, it was quick.'

He directed me to a lady in the third row. 'Who is Margaret?' I asked her.

'My mother,' she said.

'In the spirit world?'

'Yes.'

'Well, she's here too, and she wants first to speak to her granddaughter. Is that the young lady sitting next to you?'

'Yes.'

It was the mother who then took over the stage, so to speak, first addressing her granddaughter and then her daughter, and talking not only about them but other people she had known. It was almost as if the man had appeared first to introduce his wife because all the subsequent communication came from her.

She told me that her granddaughter had thought that she was rather difficult but that that was the way she had been brought up. 'We didn't show our feelings but I did love you very much,' she said, adding that the girl was like her in many ways.

'Who's Muriel?' I asked, repeating the name that I was hearing.

'An auntie,' the girl said.

'Alive?' I asked.

'Yes. My grandmother's daughter-in-law.'

'Muriel has had a tough time but your grandmother is trying to help her. Muriel didn't like her too well. That's all right, she says, she didn't like Muriel too well either!'

The audience found this rather amusing.

'She says that she learnt that you have to accept people as they come into the family. It was her son's choice, not hers, but she learnt to put up with it, and Muriel turned out better than she thought.'

'Is Muriel here?' I next asked.

'No.'

'Probably just as well,' I added, 'because she says they just couldn't communicate. Your grandmother's very dignified as she's talking to me. Oh, she says it was sometimes the same with your mother. "We were very alike," she says, "and we sparked each other off. But I was right, wasn't I?"'

'Yes,' the mother agreed.

Addressing the mother, I said: 'She's saying that she was right about what she told you in the beginning, but you were determined to do what you wanted.

'You made your bed, you had to lie on it, she says. You've got much more sensible and she's pleased, and very glad you put your foot down. You'll know what she means.

'But that's enough about you, she says. "I don't want all these people to know our business."'

There was a fair amount of laughter at this. When it had died down the daughter said: 'I hope she's happy.'

'Oh yes,' I replied, 'she says she's at peace. She couldn't wish for more than that.'

It was in Chatham that a small baby manifested herself to me. I had a feeling of pain in the head and felt that the child had died from bad breathing and perhaps jaundice. I was directed to a woman in the audience who said that she was the child's mother and that the little girl was only two days old when she had died.

'You have a son also,' I said, and the lady agreed.

Then her husband came to me and I realised that it was he who had brought the child. He told me that his wife had a pain in the chest but that she was not to worry. 'You're not coming here yet,' he told me to tell his wife.

'You also have a problem with your back and left foot,' I said. 'Your husband says they're trying to help you as much as they can.'

Then the lady's mother came, in company with a Jewish friend. They had come together to tell the lady that this year had started for her with many problems, but she would be all right by the end of the year. They also told her that she had in-law troubles but that she should not worry about them but should let them roll off her back like water.

This was not a very remarkable message in itself but it is an example of people in the spirit world seeing into the future for loved ones left behind. It is also an example of how the spirits often seem to queue up to be recognised. I first saw a lady's baby, then her husband, then her mother and then her mother's friend.

A rather more dramatic example of this also occurred that same night in Chatham. I was directed by a man from the spirit world to a lady right in front of me in the third row of the stalls. He had passed quickly, probably from a heart attack.

'Do you know who this is?' I asked.

'Yes,' the lady said.

'He says he's met your mother, who has been talking about someone called John. Do you know a John in the spirit world?'

'Yes,' the lady said again.

'John wants to be remembered to the two girls. Do you have two girls?'

'I have four.'

'Four girls?'

'That's right.'

'I wonder why he speaks about two. Do two of them have health problems?'

'No.'

'Definitely, he says that there is a health problem with one of them.'

'Yes, there is at present,' the lady said, almost as if she had just remembered.

'So he's right,' I said. 'And he's trying to help.'

I believe I was getting this message at third hand. The man who had come to me first spoke about the lady's mother and then about John, whose relationship with the lady was unclear to me, but the messages I was getting from John were passed to me by the original man.

'Who took in washing?' I suddenly asked.

'That would be my mother,' the lady said.

'Well, I'm hearing about somebody called Rose who used to bring it to the house when you were a child.'

The man then told me that the lady in the audience had a watch belonging to him which she had put on specially tonight. He had seen her at home in her apron and slippers. 'Why did she think she had to make herself look very posh for me?' he asked. He told me that he loved her very much. 'I was a bit naughty,' he admitted, 'I had to get the best of the argument but I want her to know that I always loved her.'

He then told me that the lady had some papers of his in a box in a drawer, and she agreed that this was so. 'I always gave her courage,' he said, 'and I'm at the back of her now.'

'Weren't you connected in some way with a hospital?' I asked. 'The man said he held your hand and you came out on top.'

It was only at this point, I think from listening to the tape, that I realised that the man had been the lady's husband. Usually this comes clear to me right at the start.

He suddenly started to try to pin something on me. It might have been a medal.

'Did he get a decoration?' I asked the lady.

'I don't think so,' she said.

'Wasn't he a soldier?' I said.

'That was my first husband,' was the reply.

In an instant, both husbands were there. The first husband, who had been a soldier, joined the second husband.

'I have both your husbands now,' I said, 'but just a minute. I can see three wedding rings.'

'I've only had two,' the lady said.

'I definitely see three,' I insisted.

'Don't tell me I'm going to get married again,' the lady said, much to the audience's amusement.

'Didn't you have the opportunity?' I asked.

'Yes,' was the reply, 'but he got jilted.'

And now there were three men with me. 'Good Lord,' I said, 'I have the three men who were in your life. The third one says you were the apple of his eye. You were going to be married. He regarded it as a foregone conclusion, and he considers you every bit his wife.'

I got a sudden feeling of 'puff', as I told the audience. 'I think he was shot,' was how I interpreted it.

'Yes,' the lady said. 'That's correct.'

'Never mind,' I concluded, 'the three men are telling me they have come together because they are united.'

I suppose it is a matter for comment that two husbands and a man who regarded himself as a husband should have become friends in the spirit world out of concern for the woman they had all loved and left behind.

I never knew in what circumstances the third man had been shot, but perhaps this is a good point to deal with the cases of people who died at war.

The first was a man called Robert who came to me in Glasgow with a message for his daughter-in-law. I had the strong feeling that he had been shot in the head. 'He was shot in the war,' the lady confirmed.

Robert's advice to his daughter-in-law was almost entirely how to deal with her husband, his son.

'There are problems in your marriage,' I said, to which she agreed.

'He tells me that you're the best thing that ever happened to his son, and don't let him go. He said he's weak, as weak as water, so bear with him, for his father's sake. He says you're a career girl.'

'Sort of.'

'He says you want to open a door and go out into the world. You feel trapped. Your husband trained as an artist, but he doesn't do that. Is he in the pop world?'

'He used to be.'

'I can hear pop, pop, pop. "It's a damn waste of time," Robert's saying, "that's not a real job." Does your husband do it part time?'

'Yes.'

'You often don't know where he is.'

'Very true.'

'And you told him you wouldn't share him with anybody.'

'Correct.'

'Your father-in-law says, "Give him a good pounding. You're stronger than he is. I saw you clout him right round the ear." Is that true?' I asked. 'Did you give him a good pounding?'

'Yes,' she admitted.

'Good for you,' I said, 'that's what Women's Lib is all about, but don't go too far.'

There was a certain amount of hilarity in the theatre.

'He's come, he says, because he wants to tell you that he admires you – you're a clever girl – and he thanks you for what you're doing for his son. "He doesn't deserve it," he is saying, "and I'm his father." He wouldn't tolerate his behaviour for a minute. He says – ooh, I can't say that ...'

'Go on,' the lady begged me.

'Well,' I tried to be as tactful as possible, 'while he's doing this' – and I started tapping as if with a stick – 'what is it he's doing?'

'He's a drummer,' the lady said.

'Well, while he's playing – bomp, bomp, bomp, he goes – the slightest pretty face that appears ...'

I must have stopped short. The lady obviously understood the message.

'"Tell him from me," your father-in-law says, "tell him from me to behave himself, otherwise he'll lose you." I think you've told him that already, haven't you?'

'Yes,' she said.

'He doesn't think you meant it. Make sure he does. His father says the next time it happens, give him a good punch from him!'

It was in Edinburgh that a man came to me who had

drowned during the war. I saw a small boat and a big ship, but I was slightly puzzled because he was not in uniform.

He kept telling me that the ship went down.

I went to his sister in the audience who told me that he had been one of the few survivors on the *Prince of Wales*. 'They didn't know until some time afterwards that I was on the ship,' he said.

The lady said that she was very young at the time and was not sure of the circumstances, but she knew that her brother was drowned at sea – presumably on a later occasion.

He spoke to me about Mac, Tom and Alice, all names with which his sister could identify; Alice had been his ladyfriend.

He then told me that he was now with his mother, who had died from stomach cancer, when his sister was a very little girl. She had been brought up by an older sister and they had an aunt who had been very good to them all.

The sister said that this was all true.

Her brother's final message to her was that she had had a difficult life. For twenty-five years she had been taken for a ride, but at last she had learnt to put her foot down.

A young man came to me in Harrogate and I felt that he had been shot, almost certainly in the head. He was not in uniform but I had a clear idea that he had died during the war.

I had some difficulty in tracing the person he wanted to go to but eventually a woman said that her cousin had been shot in the back of the head while he was serving with the Army in North Africa.

I was still uncertain whether the young man was directing me to her, but all became clear when a second spirit appeared whose name was Arthur. Arthur turned out to be a friend of the same lady, and it was he who had brought the boy who had been shot. The young man had wanted to come and Arthur had been able to bring him through.

The message thereafter was from Arthur, who told the lady that he had loved her but that they could not be together. Although there was no communication between them, as he put it, she was nevertheless the best thing that had ever happened to him. If things had been different, they would have been together always.

I rather feel, from hearing the tape, that the lady was somewhat surprised by this declaration of love. Her life had taken a different path and she had gone on to different things, and she certainly did not know the circumstances in which Arthur had passed, but she agreed to his request to remember him sometimes.

Then her grandmother appeared. It is obvious to me that, when I 'switch on' to somebody, particularly in these circumstances, I see other people in their lives, and that is why so often more than one spirit comes through. A communication is therefore often a very roundabout thing, as on this occasion when I started with a war victim and ended with a grandmother who told me that she had taught her granddaughter the most important values in life.

She had more valuable advice now, but suddenly she shot me across the Atlantic, as I told the lady.

'I've got friends in the US,' she said.

'Would you be surprised if you went there?' I asked.

'Yes, I would.'

'Well, don't be,' I ended on a happy note, 'because you will be going. When you get the invitation, just accept it.'

Of course the fact that somebody passes in tragic or unusual circumstances does not necessarily mean that their communications will be more interesting or more relevant than those of people who just pass quietly in their sleep of

Doris and Philip

Michael Bentine, my
great friend and
supporter *(David Willis)*

Microphones no longer bother me

At the Surrey Healers annual dinner with Angharad Rees and Christopher Cazenove

Steps in healing
(Keith Wakeley)

(Sunday Mirror)

Going to a member of the audience *(Keith Wakeley)*

A public healing on stage *(Keith Wakeley)*

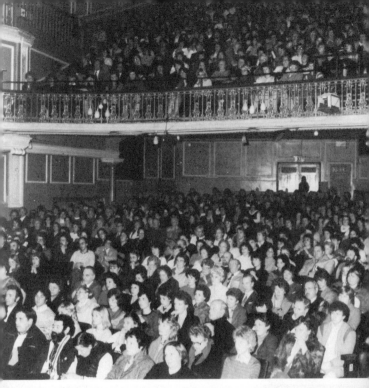

A typical
packed
audience
(Keith Wakeley)

With my
literary agent,
publisher and
manager *(Keith
Wakeley)*

Above left: With Keith, my road manager, at the close of another meeting *(Keith Wakeley)*

Above right: Outside the stage door

Below: Close rapport with the audience *(Keith Wakeley)*

old age. It just creates a slightly greater tension in the audience.

The last appearance in this series of someone who died in war never really explained itself. In the middle of a communication in Hanley from a man in the spirit world to his wife in the audience, he showed me someone who had died suddenly in the war, but this meant nothing to the wife, although I told her to go back to where she had lived as a young girl with her mother. There was insufficient recognition and I let the matter drop.

I have mentioned the matter because the rest of the message is very interesting, partly because it is so ordinary.

The man began by saying how often he had tried to get back to his wife, and she confirmed that she had never had a message before.

She had been very lonely, he told me. 'She walks from room to room and says, "Is this all my life's going to be?"'

'He says you've got courage,' I told her. 'He couldn't have managed without you but you've learned to manage without him. You've made a far better job of it than he would have done.'

Then he gave me a very clear message for his wife: 'He knows what you want,' I said, 'but you're not going to him yet. You ask how long you have got, but the answer is not yet. You've still got his chair and sometimes when you sit down, you smell him.'

'Yes,' she said.

'And you talk to him and look at the chair where he always sat. There isn't a night goes by when he doesn't say goodnight to you. And when you ask when, the answer is: not yet.'

CHAPTER 5

The Love of Humanity

Disease was on this planet before human beings. We know this by the evidence obtained from the prehistoric remains of animals. When humans emerged, they learnt to deal with pain and illness. Long before the Christian era, they were healed by non-physical methods directed towards the mind rather than the body. They wore charms for protection. Fraser's famous book *The Golden Bough* makes clear that primitive people suspected that the ills of the body were related to the mind and the soul. Modern thought has at last reached the same stage where it is believed that conditions of the mind affect the body. In ancient Greece, invalids frequented temples in the belief that the God of Medicine would cure them, while the attendant priests, many of them physicians, prepared the minds of the patients by lectures and advice. We in these modern days can readily appreciate the effectiveness of this method.

These temples were probably the first hospitals, predating the earliest Christian institutions. Perhaps the earliest known form of religious suggestion as a cure for illness was provided by the harmless yellow snakes that glided about the temples and licked the patients' sores. It was believed that since the snake was the symbol of the God of Medicine, it was the god himself who healed.

Scientific healing is usually traced back to Hippocrates, the famous Greek physician known as the father of medicine. He was born on the island of Kos off the coast of Asia Minor about 460 BC. Plato and Aristotle both referred to him with great respect. He not only made observations but recorded them, and the famous Hippocratic oath is still sworn by doctors today throughout the civilised world: 'Whatever things I see or hear concerning the life of men in my attendance on the sick, or even apart therefrom which ought not to be noised abroad, I will keep silent thereon, counting such things as to be sacred secrets.'

Jesus Christ of course was a great healer. He functioned on a high plane. He seemed to tap into energies hitherto unexplored. He was a daring healer who healed with love and also sometimes required an act of faith and mental co-operation from his patients. He appeared to teach that there is a spiritual kingdom where people may enter and where healing energies are at work more powerful than we dream of. He seemed to know the nature of a patient's trouble and why it had befallen him. Following his example, sickness became a concern of the church, and I find it sad that, perhaps because the church is no longer of one heart and mind, there has latterly been a decline in its testimony to healing.

The power of Jesus, due partly no doubt to his love for others, enriched his ability to heal.

It was well into the third century AD before the scientific methods of Greece began to percolate into Jewish practice and, to some extent, replace the amazing example of spiritual healing that was Christ's legacy to the Christian church. Methods of healing by material means came into vogue which made no demand on the faith of the patient and required no qualifications of a moral character from the healer. It is not therefore surprising that non-physical methods of healing were left behind. Drugs were now being used and their immediate success was being noted by an excited community. Men no longer beheld God working through the new methods. A drug seemed to act whether the patient believed in God or not, so healing continued only in a few monasteries, where medical manuscripts were copied and where communication was maintained with Christ and therefore his power of healing. There is no doubt that with the passing of the healing ministry, the church lost a great deal of power.

It remained for certain individuals to carry on a sequence

of healing that reaches down to the present day. We are all familiar with such names as St Francis of Assisi, Catherine of Siena, Martin Luther, George Fox and John Wesley, for example. They were all healers with no psychological technique but who healed the sick through their communion with God.

The era of the doctor arrived and church and doctor often fought a battle. In 1215 Pope Innocent III actually condemned surgery and all priests who practised it. So progress in medicine meant disassociation from the church and the two healing streams divided, never really to come together again, although I believe that in America students from the ministry can now take a course that includes an attendance at a mental hospital and under guidance can actually take charge of a case.

I do not suggest that healing through the mind can cure organic illness or take the place of surgery, but its importance in treating illness should not be underestimated. Plato recognised the influence of the mind and the emotions on physical health and that the cure of the part should not be attempted without the treatment of the whole. He believed that no attempt should be made to cure the body without the soul and therefore if the head and the body were to be well, one must begin by curing the mind. This was an early pointer to a method of healing through psychology and the astonishing thing is that apart from religious methods, no technique of healing the sick by non-physical means developed until we get to the earliest methods of using suggestion in the discovery of what was called animal magnetism. Baptista Porter used a magnet that he claimed had healing properties, but his ardour was dampened when he was accused of being a magician in league with evil spirits. Father Hell applied magnetised plates to the body but without much success. Mesmer, by his studies and procedures, formed a bridge between what he regarded as the earlier 'magical' methods and the scientific psychological methods that followed him.

Next came the hypnotic treatment of healing. James Braid, a Manchester doctor and a serious scientist, found that by fixing his eyes on those of a relaxed patient he could induce a condition that resembled sleep. He further found that in this state of induced sleep the patient exhibited characteristics that made his sleep different from the natural type, and it is to Braid that we owe the word hypnotism. He read a paper at the British Medical Association's annual congress in 1841 in which he claimed to have cured under hypnosis such afflictions as rheumatism, migraine and even paralysis. Leslie Weatherhead, in a book on religion and healing, tells us how he was able to cure a young girl of pernicious anaemia by suggesting to her mind under hypnosis that her body should manufacture red corpuscles in the normal manner. She is apparently now happily married with two children.

The Frenchman Emile Coué discovered that he had the gift of auto-suggestion. He did not require a trance state to gain access to the unconscious mind. He discovered that ideas, if repeated again and again in a confident voice when the mind is most receptive, namely at the time of waking up or falling asleep, sink into the subconscious parts of the mind. He made his patients repeat a simple slogan every morning and every evening: 'In every day in every way I am getting better.' He had outstanding success and at the height of his fame a hundred people a day thronged his garden and filled his little parlour. He knew the tremendous power of positive thought, and believed in the power of the mind over the body.

In the early years of this century, the Church of England set up a committee that advised that prayers for the restoration of health might fittingly be accompanied by the apostolic act of the laying on of hands. The poet Tennyson possessed this gift, and healed many sick people by touch.

There are innumerable other examples of healers and people who believed in their work. Mary Baker Eddy, the founder of Christian Science, was one, although I personally think that she was wrong to seek to exclude all conventional medical treatment. I prefer the example of James Moore Hickson, who actively sought the co-operation of doctors. He felt he had a definite call from God to do this work. Believing that help came definitely from the spirit, he planned a home where both spiritual and medical treatment could be given. He built a chapel and appointed a chaplain and engaged a matron and nurses, as well as the services of medical doctors, but his scheme ran foul of the General Medical Council which disapproves of doctors working alongside medically unqualified persons.

Today we have reached a point in history, brought about by these pioneers through the ages who worked and practised in completely different ways but with one common bond – the love of humanity. We too are now fighting for healers to be recognised as responsible people entitled to work in co-operation with the medical profession, not in competition with them. I know from my long personal experience that we have a major role to play, and I am pleased to say that many leading doctors agree with me.

I have observed that the deprivation of love is the main cause behind many apparently physical illnesses. The best-known case in history, I suppose, is that of Elizabeth Barrett Browning. She was dominated by a bully of a father who always found scriptural authority for his tyranny. The sensitive girl, who could not cope with a situation in which love seemed to be denied her, developed an illness that brought her a room of her own but, even more important, love, sympathy and pity. Her illness was diagnosed as consumption brought on by a fall from a horse. Doctors could not cure her but prescribed rest, quiet and good food. She suffered much pain but for twenty years led a fairly comfortable life as a chronic invalid.

Suddenly Robert Browning appeared and began to love her. She eloped with him, though she was forty years of age and he was only thirty-four, and within a year she was tramping all over the Italian mountains, and within three years she bore him a child. The illness disappeared in a night. It was not an imagined illness, nor was she feigning. I believe that her unconscious provided her with an illness as a love substitute, for it brought pity and sympathy. Unconsciously therefore she wanted to be ill and, when real love came, the illness served no further purpose and disappeared.

Healing today covers many varieties of treatment, and we speak of the holistic approach to disease. Every healer has his or her own approach to the patient. Holism comes from the Greek word for 'whole', the idea being that everything is made up of other things which are themselves wholes; for instance, water is made up of hydrogen and oxygen, two gases which have a separate existence and their own properties but which when combined together produce a substance with an independence and a characteristic of its own. This is a simple example of holistic process. The human being is much more complicated, being composed of many individual units, each with its own independence. The holistic approach therefore looks to the treatment of the whole person, and not just that of an individual part or parts. Healers and their patients must work together, because patients must learn to help themselves and not just be helped. Through thought penetration, patients can begin to take a more positive approach to their problems. I am sure many more doctors now realise the value of the whole person and know that healing does play an important part in helping patients to help themselves.

Alternative therapy, as it is sometimes called, has suddenly become respectable. It has the powerful support of Prince Charles who on more than one occasion has indicated that he regards it as an important ally of conventional medicine, not of course a replacement or substitute. Michael Meacher, as Labour spokesman on health, opened the third Alternative Medicine Exhibition and Conference in 1984. He spoke of alternative therapy as being 'the second biggest growth area in this country behind computers', and drew particular attention to acupuncture and homeopathy. 'I have seen the relief,' he said, 'afforded to my mother-in-law who suffers from a severely deteriorating spinal condition.' He welcomed the British Medical Association's investigation of the subject. 'It is time we realised,' he said, 'alternative therapy is here to stay.'

I prefer this intelligent perception to the ignorant demonstration that greeted me in Worthing by members of a local church who branded me as a dangerous force, although their minister had the grace to say, 'We do not doubt that Mrs Collins has healing powers.' He said, however, that I was in touch with evil spirits. I had earlier encountered a similar demo in Tilbury, also organised by church members, who claimed that my work – I am not sure whether they were referring to healing or clairvoyance, but I accept that they are both part of what I do – was flouting God's law, but I do not believe that such opinions of the work of spiritualists are at all widely held nowadays among churchgoers, and certainly not by most modern religious leaders.

I would refer such people to the Holy Bible. Is it not written in I Corinthians: 'To some are given the gift of speaking in diverse tongues … to some are given the gift of healing'?

I have been on both the giving and the receiving end of healing. When I had a serious operation recently, the surgeon was surprised how quickly I recovered. Having healed others, I know how healing can speed recovery. But I am not one of those who wants to work in opposition to the medical profession. As I have said so often before, I regard my work as complementary to the medical profession. When individuals approach me for healing, I always ask if they have been to their doctor. In some cases the patient has already had medical help and is seeking healing as an added boost. The doctor of today is often too burdened with forms and too busy to listen unhurriedly to a patient's problems. That is where the healer can help, if only by listening and giving the patient a feeling that somebody understands the problem, and so giving him confidence to help himself.

It is less easy to write about healing than about clairvoyance because there is far less variety, and its impact is less dramatic. I am indebted therefore to my friend, publisher Roger Schlesinger, the editor responsible for my first book, for the following brief account he has given about my work as a healer:

'I have had the privilege of watching Doris Collins demonstrate her powers of healing on several occasions whilst chairing a number of her public appearances. I am certain that these necessarily brief displays of her skills provide by no means ideal opportunities for Doris to exercise her considerable talents in this field. However, even in the five minutes or so she spends with a number of total strangers picked at random from the audience she produces some dramatic results. I remember in particular a woman of certain years hobbling up on stage with a chronic malfunction of one of her knee joints. After demonstrating that she could not bend her knee without considerable pain, Doris applied her hands to the affected area and within two minutes the jubilant woman was able to bend her knee with ease and without pain and able to walk back to her seat in the audience unaided and without a limp.

'I cannot explain in any scientific terms how Doris achieves her considerable success rate as a healer and indeed, she may not be able to do so herself. However, I am convinced that she has these powers and I can best illustrate this by recounting a healing experience I personally underwent, even though I should admit at the outset that this was only partially successful.

'Doris telephoned me one day out of the blue to tell me that she was concerned about my health. How she knew of any problem I cannot say, but I had been experiencing a bout of bronchial infection which had persisted for many weeks. She volunteered to come to my house to try healing. Within minutes of her arrival and concentrating on me, her subject, she had without any prompting "diagnosed" the few major illnesses I had had in my life. The actual conduct of the healing session consisted for the main part of close physical contact, either by holding hands or the placing of her hands on the affected area of my chest. I have never felt such heat radiated from anyone's hands before and I cannot explain this phenomenon. I had two such sessions but it was a further three weeks before my bronchial condition eased. In my opinion, therefore, I cannot necessarily claim this occurred as a direct result of Doris's work. On the other hand, one of the side effects of my illness was most definitely cured, I am convinced, due entirely to her extraordinary skills. Because of the breathing problems that were associated with my bronchitis, I had great difficulty in sleeping. On each of the two nights that followed the healing sessions,

I slept like a baby and thereafter until my chest cleared I had
no more interrupted nights.

'This short personal case history may convince no one of
Doris's healing powers, but something phenomenal happened to me which convinced me that she has a gift that few
possess and, as a doctor's son, I had as much reason as
anyone to be sceptical.'

I treasure this tribute from an intelligent person whose
health improved as a result of my healing. I can only go by
what I am told. In my last book I quoted famous dancer and
mime artist Adam Darius whom I had treated. He was
apparently so impressed that when he injured his back in
Italy he telephoned me from Turin where he was due to give
two performances at the Teatro Nuovo. 'My back is
paralysed,' he told me. 'I can't even bend down to take my
shoes off.' He said he would have to cancel his appearances
and return the tickets.

'No, you will perform,' I told him. According to his
account, I cured him over the telephone. I asked him to try
to bend down and touch the floor with his hands, and to his
amazement he was able to do so. 'It was a miracle,' he says,
'I could actually do it with my knees straight!' He woke up
the next morning however in some pain, perhaps because
the mattress was too soft. He rang me again and I gave him
more telephonic healing. 'Throughout the day,' he says, 'I
found it easy to bend down, and that evening I gave an
almost perfect performance.'

To those readers who have not read my earlier book, I
should perhaps here repeat that on occasion I have had
excellent results with absent healing – in other words with
healing at a distance. Very few healers are clairvoyant, and
not all clairvoyants can heal, so there is not necessarily any
connection between the two gifts. I happen to be both a
clairvoyant and a healer, and I use the two gifts – and also

auric vision, about which I shall have something to say shortly – hand in hand. This may help to explain the possibility of healing somebody over the long-distance telephone.

In my first book I told the story of how I helped the famous New Zealand runner, John Walker, at a critical time in his career. Since then I have sought to heal another athlete, a young tennis player called Tony Mitchell, whose trainer heard about me either from John Walker or from someone who knew about the matter. This young lad had been a champion junior tennis player and had gone to America for training. Sadly, he suffered a severe arm injury that put paid to his tennis for two years, during which time he had all sorts of treatment, including three serious operations on his wrist.

I was asked to see Tony and in fact we had seven meetings. After the third, he was able to start playing tennis again, and at the end of our sessions he was playing four or five hours a day.

He has kept in touch with me on and off ever since. The healing was partly physical and partly mental, because I was able to restore his confidence. I was very thrilled recently when he telephoned me from Florida to report progress, and I could not possibly have any greater joy than to hear that he succeeds in his chosen sport. I should love him to get to the top but the fact that he is playing at all is reward enough for what little I was able to do for him.

I do not have time to follow up the many people I heal on stage for a few minutes, and I have to rely on their testimony, when available, as to the efficacy of my work. I get a lot of letters from people to whom I have given healing, and most of them speak well of my efforts. Sometimes, if I look at reports in the local newspapers in towns where I have appeared, I read statements from people who claim to have benefited from my treatment, if that is the right word. There was for example the lady in Swansea who told a reporter that she had suffered for years with arthritis. 'Doris relaxed me,' she said. 'I felt a surge of power shoot through my body. Suddenly I could move my neck and arms without pain. It's a long time since I have been able to do that.'

It sounds big-headed always to be praising myself but I do not know how else to write about healing, which is so very important to me, without reporting what people say about me. If they all seem so supportive, I can only say so. Perhaps my failures do not bother to waste a stamp on me!

I will end this chapter by quoting two letters that I received with great joy. I have selected them from a large number of similar letters because they strike me as being of interest. The first is from a lady in Zurich. I am sure she will not mind if I slightly improve her English.

'I am writing you,' she said, 'regarding my sister Frieda. She had poliomyelitis when she was seven years old. Her age is now thirty-six and I took her along to you about two years ago and asked you to give her some force and energy, as she was often depressed and was always at home with my parents.

'After you gave her a treatment, she could bend her right knee, which she had not been able to do for over thirty years. As I live on the fifth floor without a lift, I asked my sister to climb up step by step. She looked at me with big eyes and told me that she had never done anything like that before, but I told her to do so and it really worked.'

In the same letter the lady writes that although her sister may not always be thinking of me at nine, she does so on her behalf. This is a reference to the fact that I ask all my patients to think of me every evening at nine o'clock whenever possible. I myself think of them at that hour whenever I am in a position to do so. Of course I cannot think of them individually but I send out absent healing en masse, and I believe that it can have a beneficial effect. For those people whom I have only seen once, it is a form of continuing healing and contact with me.

The day would not be long enough to see all the people who contact me for healing, either for themselves or for someone they love. The best I can do is to put their names in what I call an Absent Healing Book and think about them each evening when I am able to do so at nine o'clock. Even those who doubt if there can be much good in my sending out healing thoughts will probably agree that it can be a comfort to a sick or disabled person to know that someone is thinking of them at a particular time.

Perhaps that is what the lady meant who wrote to me from Brixham to say that I give many people 'renewed hope'. She had been a nun for ten years before she decided that her life was meant to take a different direction.

This lady, whose name is Margaret, came to see me in Paignton. She was deaf, and I cured her, she said. 'Having completed the medical circuit both here and in America,' she wrote, 'my condition was marked "incurable" on all the records.'

'You may laugh,' she continued, 'when I tell you what a great joy it is for me just to hear my eardrums pop and to be aware of the little sounds that everyone takes for granted. Every day I have a miracle, every time I hear a whisper, every moment free of pain. I thank God for His love and yours.'

Last Christmas I received a card from Margaret, inside which she enclosed a photograph of herself. She has a very attractive, happy face. On the back of the photo are the words: 'Yes, Doris, I can hear.'

CHAPTER 6

The Aura

I once took orange marigolds to a patient in hospital. The surgeon happened to come in while I was there. 'What lovely flowers,' he said. 'I wonder if you know the value of orange. It is a great healing colour.' What the surgeon did not know is that I had chosen the flowers deliberately, partly because of their colour, because I was aware that the patient needed to respond confidently to her situation.

I dislike giving clairvoyance in a very red room because bright red over-stimulates me. I have heard it said that some drivers of bright red cars are very pushy, on the same theory, whereas some colours have a soothing quality.

I have always been conscious of the value of colour, and indeed I have used auric vision in my work. Not all clairvoyants see the aura that surrounds people. I always have, but not all the time.

When I am concentrating on clairvoyance, I do not find auric vision very useful, but I sometimes find it very helpful in healing, particularly when dealing with someone with emotionally disturbed feelings. The colours surrounding people tell me a great deal about them. They change all the time. To use orange again as an example, it is a sign of intellectual activity when seen round the head. If someone is concentrating on a mental problem, his head may be aglow with orange, which will decrease in density or even disappear entirely when his mind relaxes. A terrible shock can completely alter one's aura. When healing, I sometimes diagnose by observing changing colour and density in the auric field. I know it sounds a silly thing to say, but I sometimes seem to feel colour through my hands.

I have been asked so often over the years to explain what is meant by the aura that I have decided to say a few words about it here. Readers who find it difficult are advised to go to the next chapter.

The human body is surrounded by a magnetic field that

increases or decreases in changing environments. Just as the earth has a polarity between north and south, so polarity exists between the feet and the head. Animals can sense danger through this magnetic field but we humans have lost a great deal of the awareness through the process of civilisation. Every form of life has its radiation.

The aura is composed of various levels, each representing a part of our nature. It is seen as a luminous colour surrounding the body and those who have studied these matters have become convinced by experience that we possess not only a physical body but a more refined spiritual body also. In old occult writings, this was referred to as the astrobody, but in different parts of the world and at different times it has gone under other names. Nowadays it is often called the etheric body.

Many old teachers believed that the etheric body draws vital energy from the sun which is radiated in a haze that extends all round the physical body. In highly developed people, this haze can extend many feet.

The aura at all times registers our emotions and mental state, but the general colouring alters slowly as our feelings, thoughts and physical condition change.

The etheric body is closely linked with the physical body and many clairvoyants actually see them linked by a silver cord, which is broken when death comes and the spirit leaves the physical body. I have seen this once myself, when I was sitting with a person who died while I was in the room. Once the cord is broken, there can be no return. This corresponds exactly in part with the words in the Bible, in Ecclesiastes: 'Or ever the silver cord be loosed ... then shall the dust return to the earth as it was; and the spirit shall return unto God who gave it.'

Just before the First World War a book called *The Human Atmosphere* was written by Dr W. J. Kilner of St Thomas's

Hospital in London. In it he announced that he had discovered a method whereby the human aura could be observed. He realised that if magnetic radiations were perceptible to specially sensitive people, they belonged to the order of phenomena known as ultra-violet because this type of light is normally invisible to sight, being on too short a wavelength or too high a frequency for ordinary vision. So it occurred to him that if the aura was a reality, it should be possible to construct some kind of apparatus to exclude light rays and to render visible the ultra-violet. He was so sure of this that he threw himself into his research and after several years perfected a screen. I do not want to go into technical detail in a book of this sort but as a result of his work, he and his associates found that a human being is entirely surrounded by a faint luminous mist, somewhat oval in shape, and usually extending about eighteen inches to two feet in all directions.

It is said that there are seven centres in the body – about the head, between the eyes, the throat, the heart, the spleen, the base of the spine and the solar plexus – which distribute energy to all other centres.

With this in mind, Dr Kilner began to apply his knowledge to methods of diagnosing disease and in 1919 he formulated a system of auric diagnosis. He discovered that peculiarities in certain auras, especially in women, could be changed at will, causing rays to issue from the body or the colour of the aura to alter.

He wrote extensively about the aura and he realised that the etheric body is the centre or vehicle of the vital sources in the body and thus of paramount importance as regards health. A healthy etheric body stores up an abundance of vital force that radiates in straight lines in every direction. When we are sick the etheric body is unable to draw the same amount of force and the magnetic lines appear feeble and bent.

Dr Kilner created and marketed goggles which he claimed could enable one to see the aura. I have never used them myself because fortunately I can see the aura without any need of physical help. Rays affect the entire universe, as Dr Kilner knew. Science has discovered a great deal about rays; we have the X-ray, the violet ray, the ultra-violet ray and the infra-red ray, but little is known about the cosmic ray. Rays are really manifestations of different rates of vibration, and I prefer to use the word 'vibration' because I think it best describes the phenomenon. Colour is vibration. The world of nature is a symphony of colour, varying from the delicate hues of the dawn, through the gleaming intensity of the midday sun in summer, to the vivid tints of sunset.

It has been said that there are seven basic types of human temperament which in turn are reflected by seven major vibratory colours – violet, indigo, blue, green, yellow, orange and red. I have not myself been able to catalogue the different types of human mentality, but I certainly know that these colours dominate the aura.

Let me start with red. It is a very visible colour and a symbol of life. A great deal of red in a person's aura denotes strength and vitality. People with a lot of red have very strong physical propensities, minds and wills but usually also a rather materialistic outlook on life. They are often very warm and affectionate people, full of love and courage.

Orange expresses the vital force. It represents the force of the sun, what yogis call the soul of energy, and the presence of strong orange hues in the aura shows a personality that is vital, energetic and active. Orange people are usually very live wires and they very often dominate their fellows by sheer force of their vital qualities. They are born for positions of responsibility and they find it much easier to rule than to

serve. They are also very good masters because they are
tactful managers and mix very well with all classes of
people.

Yellow denotes soul qualities, the astromental forces. It
symbolises thought and mental concentration, and is a
stimulating colour for health and mental activity. It is a
colour associated with the need for intellectual stimulation.
It signifies light, also representing the sun, and bright
golden yellow has a spiritual significance that accounts for
its frequent use in religious ceremonies. Golden vessels and
yellow altar fittings are very common. I believe that yellow
roses can be most beneficial. They possess the power to
dispel worry.

We have all heard of the green eye, and people with green
in their aura can be envious and jealous, but by and large it
is a good colour, representing individuality. Green governs
individual growth and people who have achieved a great
deal of success in life invariably display a green tint in their
aura. Like yellow, green also governs our mental capabili-
ties. Green people are versatile, thoughtful and adaptable.

Blue represents inspiration. It is a very spiritual colour,
and the darker the blue, the more likely it is that a person is
wise and saintly. The presence of a great deal of blue in the
aura signifies a very harmonious, artistic and spiritual
understanding. It is a vibration associated with the moon
and with feminine aspects, and denotes self-reliance and
competence.

Indigo in the aura often shows a high degree of sensuality
and integrity.

Violet is rarely seen in the average aura. It is also a highly
spiritual colour. Indeed it hardly belongs to the earth plane
but to a high sphere of spiritual beings. It has long been
regarded as a royal colour, a colour of power and influence,

and its presence in the aura usually denotes true greatness and worthiness.

Then we get to the in-between colours. There is grey, which is neither white nor black. Its presence in a person's aura usually indicates a lack of imagination and a tendency to be very narrow-minded, although some observers associate it with concentration and perseverance. Grey people are certainly very persistent, but I find that they are mostly plodding types, lone wolves or people who want to do everything their own way.

I have never found a great deal of black in a person's aura, perhaps because it is a negation of colour. Historically it has been associated with dark deeds, so perhaps most of the people I meet are basically good.

The ancient philosophers regarded pink as a mystic colour but to me it denotes a quiet, modest type of character. Very rarely do we see pink in the aura of positive, dogmatic people. It is much more likely to be found in those who like a quiet life and are fond of artistic things and beautiful surroundings.

Silver people are often lively and volatile, but sometimes a little unreliable. The colour goes with people who are versatile, active and gifted in matters pertaining to movement, speech and travel. Sometimes they are dabblers in all trades or professions but are masters of none. Like quicksilver, they never seem to stay still or settle down.

People with much brown in their aura have a great capacity for organisation and orderly management. It is the colour of the businessman or executive and for workers in industry. They are rarely people of strong emotional feelings or tendencies. They are usually somewhat conventional, with apple-pie types of mind, but that does not stop them from being ambitious for power and money, and they have a great deal of perseverance.

Of course, I have only given a shorthand impression of what colour indicates to me when I use auric vision. It is much more complicated than this, and the aura consists of many colours simultaneously, one melting into another. There is usually, however, an overall basic colour surrounding an individual and I have found it an excellent guide to a person's character. Allied to my psychic gift, it could be a powerful help, but I have explained that I rarely use it except for healing, perhaps because I do not really need it in my clairvoyance. To some extent I heal clairvoyantly but I definitely find auric vision of value in my healing. It can be very helpful to assess how best to help sick people from observation of the colours surrounding them.

I know that many people will disagree with my somewhat simplistic diagnosis of the aura, but I have explained what it means to me and what each colour represents to me.

CHAPTER 7

They Are Not Dead

Because most people pass into the spirit world in old age, or following an illness, it does not make their attempts to communicate with the living any less important; but of course, as I have said before, there is always additional drama when someone has passed more violently or unnaturally, as for example in an accident.

It is one thing to die after a long lifespan; quite another to have one's life cut short in youth or middle age. Hence there is likely to be more tension in an audience when messages come from people whose natural lives were cut short.

A young man appeared to me in Margate who had a message for his mother in the audience. He had died in an accident and I had the impression that something had dropped on him or hit him.

His mother confirmed that her son had been killed following a crash between a car and a motorcycle.

'He was shot into the air,' I said. 'Was he twenty-three?'

'No, twenty,' his mother replied.

The boy sent a message to his mother about her back, saying that it would be all right in due course. Then he had something to say to someone called Mick. 'Tell him it's not so bad here,' were his words, 'I'm okay.'

As so often happens when I am talking to a particular person, I become involved clairvoyantly with the person next door, or sometimes with several people nearby. On this occasion I received messages for the man next to the lady to whom I had been speaking. I am not sure whether they were related in any way or if they were sitting next to each other by chance.

'Do you work in metal?' I asked.

'Yes,' the man said.

Eventually his mother came through. He told me that she had been a medium.

'Your mother wants to put something round your neck,' I said.

'Probably a rope,' he laughed, and the audience joined in.

'More likely it's a tie,' I said. 'Oh yes, you got one out and then put it back.'

'That's right,' he said, 'earlier today.'

I should perhaps say here that that is not very remarkable because many men select and then reject a tie when dressing, but I am sure I must have felt the woman trying to put something round my neck.

This particular message concluded by the woman confirming her son's belief that she was a medium. 'I'm coming back because I want him to be happy,' she told me.

'Three years ago,' I told the man, 'you went to hospital. It was touch and go, but your mother helped you. She says she's not ready for you yet.'

The following night in Bristol, another young man came to me who had died in an accident. He too had a message for his mother.

Funnily, I asked her the same question I had put to the boy's mother in Margate: 'Was he twenty-three?' Apparently I was a year out because he had been twenty-four when he passed.

'Your son says he has tried to get through to you before,' I told his mother, 'but it hasn't been possible. Something hit him. I think it was a car. He said, "It hit me like a steamroller." What was it?'

'A Transit van,' the lady said.

'Was he walking?'

'He was hitch-hiking.'

'He says you told him not to do it, so many times.'

'Yes, but every time he did it.'

'He's telling me they laid him at the side of the road,' I said. 'They put something under his head. It was all over in a few minutes. You went to see him in hospital. You kissed him and said he was going to live. He says not to worry: he's all right.'

Then I asked if the lady had two daughters, which she said was true, because her son was sending them his love.

'You've got his picture in your bag,' I went on. 'In fact you've got it on you now.'

'Yes,' she said.

'You've had his picture enlarged, and when you walk in the room, he's the first person you see. He used to say you were pretty.'

'Yes.'

'He says, "You still are, Mum. You still look as pretty as ever."'

Had I been trying to create an effect, I could hardly have succeeded better, but that was certainly not my intention. In fact it cannot have been my intention because when I am giving clairvoyance, I am unaware of surrounding circumstances; or at most I am only vaguely aware.

It is not surprising that the lady should have wept at this lovely but emotional message from her son, but I am sure the audience were in sympathy with her and sharing her experience, so it should not have been embarrassing.

When she had recovered, I continued. 'Your son says, "Just say Pat." Who's Pat?'

'That's me,' the lady said.

'He said, "Pat's got pretty feet and don't wear those awful boots!"'

This message seemed to relax the tension.

'Do you do a job with your fingers?' I next asked.

'Yes,' the lady said, 'I serve fish and chips.'

'That's why you wear those boots,' I said, although I am not sure what her son can have meant by telling me that.

'You haven't always done that job,' I said, 'and you're

waiting to get out of it. You will. Your son says not to worry. They're helping you. Just float on the wind.'

I pause here for a brief moment to say that this is one of literally thousands of examples of people in the spirit world saying that they are helping, or trying to help, their loved ones. Perhaps none of us is really alone.

The young man then spoke about a friend called Graham who had a motorbike and lived two streets away and another friend called Alan. Then he said something quite extraordinary for a young man.

'He's said, "Mary, Mary, quite contrary, How does your garden grow?" Do you understand that?'

'No,' the lady replied.

'He says you do understand. You like flowers. What's the problem with the garden?'

'I never do it. Dad does it,' she said.

'He says give Dad a hand. Is Dad here?'

'Yes.'

'He asks Dad to say hullo to Bob. Who's that?'

'His friend,' the father said.

'You've had a bit of trouble with your back,' I told him. 'That's because Mum doesn't help you with the garden. Your son says you had problems with your hair.'

'Yes.'

The boy's final message for his parents was most interesting. 'This is the first time I've come back and I'm so happy,' he said – 'and,' he added, 'I'M NOT DEAD!'

A young girl who had died following a car accident came to me in Paignton. She spoke about two other girls called Maisie and Vicky. 'There were three of us together,' she said, 'and I ran across the road.' The other girls screamed, she told me.

A woman in the audience identified herself as Vicky.

'She says the accident didn't kill her,' I told her. 'She was taken to hospital and then she died.'

Vicky agreed that this was true.

'At school,' I went on, 'you had a teacher and she had a very large chest. She had a row of beads and every time she walked, they "bomped". She was a bit like a sergeant major. They were amber, yellowy beads. She says she's got to tell you this so you know it's her. Now she says you're not Vicky at all. You're Victoria.'

'That's correct.'

'She used to call you Queen Victoria, just for a lark. She says you've got specs on but you didn't wear them when she knew you. She says she's glad she's come back. You were her friend. Thank you, Victoria, she said, for listening to her.'

This may not be as dramatic and authoritative a message as the last but it is remarkable for the detail by which the girl sought to be identified beyond mistake.

Even a small child can help us from the spirit world if the next message is to be believed. It seems very much as though families stick together there, perhaps even more closely than they do on the earth plane.

It was in Ayr that a small boy came to me who had been run over by a car. I went to a woman in the audience who was connected with him, but I am not certain of their relationship. I was able to tell her that the last two years of her life had not been easy for her and that the child was doing everything he could to help her.

The boy was accompanied by a gentleman who had passed quickly. 'This is your grandfather,' I told the lady. 'He says be patient and don't change anything. You have three children?'

'Yes.'

'And with one of them you have problems with discipline and of how to give it?'

'Yes.'

'Well, he says you must, and then things will be better at home.'

If the boy was the woman's son, then the man he brought along was presumably his great-grandfather whom he would almost certainly never have known in this life.

A man came to me in Preston with messages for his mother and sister in the audience, but it was principally the sister whom he wanted to contact.

'I have come to give my sister help,' he said. 'She's had a very difficult life.' And he told me that, among her other problems, she had lost twin boys and a little girl the previous year.

'Are you divorced?' I asked her.

'No,' she said.

'Separated?' I persisted.

'Yes.'

'Same thing,' I said, 'to your brother. Well, as soon as you get that cleared up, the better. You've got something wrong with your arm?'

'Yes. It was injured in a road accident.'

'Oh yes, you and your brother were together. "But she survived," he says, "and I was wiped out!" He says you're too depressed. Pull yourself together and weather the storm. Don't worry about your husband. He was never any good anyway. Stop crying, he's not worth it. "I've come back," your brother says, "to give you courage and help."'

This theme of making contact in order to help recurs in hundreds of messages. There were two examples the following night in Gateshead.

I first saw a young man of about nineteen who was asking for his mother, but I was directed to his sister in the audience.

'I feel this young man was hit in the chest,' I said. 'I feel a pain there. What hit him?'

'A lorry,' she said. 'He was running.'

'Yes, I feel it was something heavy. I feel completely crushed. He says, "I want my mother." '

'I've come on her behalf,' the young lady said, 'she's in hospital.'

'Is she having an operation?' I asked.

'No, it's a nervous breakdown. She gave me an object that was on his body when he died.'

'He's only been dead two months,' I said, 'he was two weeks away from being nineteen. He's talking about three o'clock, three o'clock.'

'That was the time of his death.'

'He wants his mother to know he's all right,' I said.

'That's why she's in hospital,' the girl said, 'because of the accident.'

'He's mentioned David and Richard and various people and he wants them all to know he's all right. His mother is in hospital because of the shock but she'll be all right too. He wants to tell his mother not to blame anyone. "It was my fault," he says, "I took a chance and the lorry hit me. Tell my mum her prayers have been answered." '

My next communication followed on directly from the last. 'This lad,' I said, 'has brought another boy who was killed, but this boy has been in the spirit world longer.'

This shows that people make new friends in the spirit world, just as they do on earth.

I went to a woman who identified her son.

'He's been dead longer,' I said.

'Yes, eighteen months.'

'He says he was very naughty to have done what he did. He took a chance. How old was he?'

'Twenty-three.'

'He says he wanted the car.'

'But he wasn't driving.'

'Were there two others with him?'

'Yes.'

'He said he larked about and was full of fun. He was very adventurous.'

He then told me that his mother had had a rough time for the last two years and that he wanted to help her.

'He wants also to say hullo to his sister.'

'That's Pauline,' the mother said. 'She's here with me.'

'Did he call her Paula?'

'Sometimes.'

'Yes, that's right. He only did it because she hated it, he says.'

There was laughter at that.

'Let me speak to Pauline,' I said. 'Your brother says, "I know I teased you, but I didn't mean it. I did love you very much. You were the best sister a boy could have." No tears, he says. Good Lord, he says you've seen him since he passed, and he spoke to you.'

'Yes.' she agreed. 'I sensed him in my little boy's bedroom.'

'Yes,' I said, 'out of the blue you saw him. You couldn't believe it and you told your mother. "I tried to get close," he says, "for you to tell my mother I was all right." '

In Derby a boy of about eight appeared and I went to a woman in the balcony. The child was her late husband's brother and he told me that he had been brought by Bill, who was the lady's uncle.

I told the lady that the boy kept tugging at my side as if to pull me away from something. 'How was this boy killed?' I asked her. 'I know it was a terrible accident.'

'A train ran into him,' she replied.

That explained the tugging. 'He was on the line,' I said, 'crossing where he shouldn't have been.'

'"I was very naughty," the boy told me. "Those lines had such a fascination for me." He loved trains. They drew him. He had to go. He thought he'd just make it but the train hit him. It didn't just hit him. Oh dear, I have a feeling that it cut him in half!'

'Yes, that's right,' the lady said.

'"You've told my mother I'm not dead," the boy says, "but she doesn't believe you. My mother never got over it. I was her favourite. My other brother's grown up now, and she still says, 'If only your brother was alive today.' Well, tell her I'm so sorry I was so naughty and I gave her so much grief and so many problems."'

I later learnt from the local newspaper that this accident had occurred twenty-five years before. The lady to whom the message was addressed had come to my meeting, hoping to hear from her husband. Instead she received a message from his brother. 'It was all true,' she told the reporter. 'I felt a presence as if someone was brushing me.'

Yet another child who was killed manifested himself to me in Sheffield. I told the audience that he could not speak to his mother because she did not believe in the possibility of life after death, so I went instead to an aunt.

The boy had died at the age of thirteen and his name was Michael.

'He ran into the road,' I said.

'Yes,' the aunt acknowledged.

'Did he have a little bicycle?'

'Yes.'

'He left the bicycle and ran into the road.'

'Yes.'

'His mother cut a piece of his hair off before he was buried.'

'Yes, that's right.'

'He says, "Tell my mum and my sister that I'm all right."'

This constant effort to reassure the living that they need not worry about the dead is an ever-present theme in these messages.

It surprises me when I read the transcripts how many children, some little more than babies, come through who have been accident victims. Yet another came to me in Birmingham. This was a little girl aged three who asked for her mother. The child told me that her mother had had a second baby.

'Yes, I had two children,' the lady said, 'but not at the same time.'

'But you lost them both.'

'Yes, I did.'

The rest of this communication came from the lady's husband's grandmother, who said that she had got the babies with her in the spirit world.

An even younger child, aged two, came to me in Harlow, and I went to his aunt in the audience.

'I have a boy and I think he was drowned,' I said. 'I feel water passing over me. He wasn't very old.'

'Only two,' the aunt said.

'He was with three children.'

'Yes, my two daughters and his sister.'

'Somehow I got the impression of still water. I didn't think I was in the sea.'

'Yes, it was still water. It was a swimming pool.'

'He gave me the feeling of struggling for his life and going down. Did he fall in?'

'We don't know that. We don't know if someone pushed him or not.'

'I think he had his clothes on.'

'He did.'

'Because he's coming here and I felt he had a little pair of trousers on and a shirt.'

'That's right. Yes.'

'And he said to me, "I didn't do it. I wasn't naughty."'

'He wasn't. He was good,' the aunt agreed.

'He's talking about Rose.'

'That's right.'

'Who's Rose?'

'That's his sister.'

'Yes, Rose or Rosie. He says, "Say hullo to her." And he's talking about Ann, or could it be Pam?'

'That's his mum, my sister Pam.'

'He says he wants to talk to his mum but she's not here, and she wouldn't believe. He says would you tell her that he has been back?'

The child then started talking about March. 'It's important to his mother, he said.'

His aunt said that March was the father's birthday but she could not think of anything else significant about the month.

'There's a bit of a problem with Dad,' I said.

'Yes, he's just had an operation.'

'He said, "Will you tell Mummy I'm helping with Dad as much as I can."'

This remark interests me considerably because it shows that even the youngest spirits can try to help us, and I think it obvious that there must be a development in the spirit world because no child of two could possibly communicate in such a fashion on the earth plane.

As I told the aunt, I was told by the child that the father's operation was 'rather nasty'. 'He hasn't got over it yet but he will.'

Then the child's grandmother came to me suddenly. 'Oh, Grandma's come,' I told the audience.

'That'll be my mum,' the lady said.

'He said to me, "My grandma has brought me." Now who's Arthur? Your mother's talking about Arthur.'

There was no response.

'He's someone your mother has met in the spirit world. Don't look for a relative. I want to take you back to when you were a girl because she's showing me here a row of houses. Do you know anything about Stanley Road or Stanley Street? Or Stanley Grove?'

'That's where we used to live,' the lady said.

'She's saying it, you see. That's where you used to live as a girl?'

'That's right.'

'She's talking about – oh, I missed it – I thought she said 37.'

This brought no reaction.

'Was it 73?' I wondered.

'That was the shop we used to live in.'

'Because she's repeated it, you see. She wrote it up for me. Why is she talking about the greengrocer's?'

The lady's reply is unclear on the tape but what is clear is that a greengrocer's had a significance for her.

'Why is she talking about Tottenham?' I next asked.

'That's where my mum comes from.'

'She says, "I'm glad to come back and talk to you because it makes us one united family."'

We never did learn who Arthur was but I am quite certain that he was someone close to the lady's mother. She could hardly have been wrong about that and right about so much else, down to the smallest detail of an address.

Yet another child aged two appeared in Oxford. She had drowned, 'I think,' I said, 'in a river, not the sea.'

This child went to her grown-up sister in the audience

and sent a message to another sister, Mary. 'She said there were five of them together,' I said.

'That's right,' the lady agreed.

'She said she was after a piece of wood. She went to get the wood and fell in. The boy, she says, tried to get her but she was carried away. They found her – I think after three days.'

'No, at three o'clock,' her sister said.

'Ah yes, that's right. Her mother's with her. She is dead now too. She's holding her hand. The child says, "If only my mother had been there, it wouldn't have happened."'

Studying these tapes, it is quite astonishing that the vast majority of people who came to me after passing in an accident were young. Many were babies or little children, and very few were older than their early twenties. Perhaps these youngsters have a greater need to communicate, or perhaps they recognise that the people they left behind need their comfort and reassurance all the more because they lost dear ones at such a tender age.

I shall give one further example, which also occurred that same night in Oxford. This was another young person, although not another baby.

'I have a girl,' I said, 'who passed quickly. She wants her mum. It was about three years ago.'

I was directed to a woman in the audience whom I knew at once was the mother in question.

'Was it an accident?' I asked.

'Yes.'

'Were there two people knocked down, but she was the only one who was killed?'

'Yes.'

'Who's Jane?'

'My sister.'

'She wants to say hullo to her. She was fond of Jane.'

Then I told the mother that her daughter had only

survived a short time. They had tried to save her life and her mother had hardly ever left her side. 'But she says she knew, and she thinks you knew, she wouldn't make it. She was unconscious.'

'She was unconscious for seven weeks,' her mother said.

This is not what I would have called a short time, but that was what the girl had told me.

'Yes, she was unconscious, she says, but she knew you were there,' I told the mother.

'Was she nineteen?' I asked.

'It was on her seventeenth birthday but she would have been nineteen now.'

'She tells me she was crossing over, and she said something about the grass.'

'She was run down on the pavement.'

' "They laid me on the side," she says. A policeman rolled up a coat and put it under her head. It was so soft. Then she lost consciousness.'

Then the girl said something really extraordinary. 'I want you to know that my spirit left my body three days before my heart stopped.'

Through me, she told her mother: 'I saw you sitting there, two women and a man. I was over the top of the bed and I saw you.'

'Her father was there,' I said.

'Yes,' her mother replied.

I knew that two of the people the girl had seen were her parents but I did not pursue the matter further and try to identify the other woman. It may have been a friend or a nurse, not necessarily a close relation.

The girl then left a message for her father, of whom she was very fond, she said. He had been very good with money. 'When I died,' she said, 'I owed him some. Say thank you to him because I've never been able to pay him back.'

CHAPTER 8

While There Is Death,
There Is Hope

I have explained how people whose lives have been cut short by fatal accidents seem to line up to communicate with their loved ones. The urge to communicate must be even stronger for people who have taken their own lives deliberately. They seem to need to explain their desperate acts and to apologise for the trouble they caused to those they left behind.

Sixteen people who had committed suicide appeared to me on my month-long series of meetings, a smaller number of course than those who had died from illness or as a result of accident; but a high number, I suspect, if one relates the incidence of suicide to other causes of death.

On an earlier tour, four cases of suicide were reported in the newspapers. A Chinese woman, for example, came to me in the audience and mentioned the name Mr Chou, which triggered off messages about a series of events that the woman understood perfectly.

Then there was the man in Buxton who had hanged himself outside his bedroom. I went directly to the family concerned in the theatre.

In Worthing I received a message for a man in the audience whose mother-in-law had killed herself. She told him that he would marry his girlfriend, who was living with him, and that only then would his ex-wife leave him alone. He was amazed at what he recognised as the accuracy of the communication.

I shall not go into any details about these messages because they were not tape-recorded, but before dealing further with the tapes, I must refer to what seems to be a somewhat unusual double communication that occurred at Wimbledon in South London. My literary agent took the chair for me that night and so has been able to give a personal impression of what happened. Apparently two people who had died by their own hands tried to communicate through me with members of the audience simultaneously.

'Any message,' he writes, 'is dramatic, even a funny one, and Doris's programme, if that is the right word, is a mixture of laughter and tears. She can be very, very funny at one minute and extremely dramatic the next. There is a curious blend of sentiment and practical advice. She can be tough at times, like a headmistress admonishing a naughty child, when she has to deliver a very direct and positive message, and then she will switch in an instant to a sympathetic, caring personality when the message is consoling.

'Doris is a large lady with a very strong presence, and she can be formidable at times. This is not the real Doris because something takes over when she is demonstrating clairvoyance. The real Doris is a practical, quiet and sympathetic lady, and these qualities are revealed at other times during her clairvoyance and at all times while she is healing.

'An evening with Doris Collins on stage is a cathartic experience that one only gets from great theatre, but Doris is not an actress. However professionally presented, she remains essentially an amateur, and I believe that it would ruin her successful impact to try to change her. What she does comes naturally and cannot be stage-managed.

'I have the advantage of having studied her at work on many occasions. She has a number of "tricks", not in the sense that a magician has, but little means of establishing quick contact with people in the audience. There is certainly no cheating involved.

'I know that the messages she receives vary in clarity. She may think she hears the name Don when in fact she should have heard Ron, and sometimes the message she passes on is not understood, or misunderstood. But so very often she hits the nail bang on the head in a manner that is decisive.

'After all is said and done, it seems to me that there is in Doris's work a kernel of irrefutable truth. However sceptical one may be, I do not think it is possible for a fair-minded person to leave a theatre with a closed mind after watching Doris demonstrate.

'In any case her sheer theatrical impact is astonishing. I witnessed this when I chaired a meeting for Doris at the Wimbledon Theatre, when two people who had committed suicide seemed to be fighting for her attention.

'Doris apparently felt someone put a cord or whatever around her neck, and she was suddenly seen to be struggling to release her neck from its grip. "Oh dear," she said, "I have someone here who hanged himself. He's putting something round my neck." This I understand to be a frequent means by which a spirit will identify himself who has died in this manner. Then while she was still almost tottering on the stage and holding her neck, she said, "I can't breathe. I can smell gas. I thought he had hanged himself but I'm not sure that he didn't put his head in the oven."

'All became clear a few moments later when Doris regained control of the situation. A man who had hanged himself wanted to communicate with his wife in the audience and at the same time a woman who had gassed herself was trying to contact her family. They both had such an urgent need to get through that they were fighting with Doris for attention.

'Doris dealt with the situation splendidly. Having recovered her equilibrium, she was at her most magisterial as she told the man to stand aside. "I'll come back to you later," she said, "I'll deal with the lady first."

'That is exactly what she did. The gassed lady and the hanged man came through in turn to explain the circumstances in which they had killed themselves – "I couldn't face life any longer," the man said, and "I warned you before

I was going to do it but you didn't believe me," were the woman's words – and both asked their people in the audience to try to understand and to forgive them for the sorrow they had caused.

'The sheer drama of this double encounter was one of the most moving experiences I had ever had in a theatre, and it was a relief indeed when the next message was for a young girl, advising her which of two boyfriends to marry.'

My literary agent has asked me to say that he did not take notes at the time but has written the above events from memory.

Returning to the tapes, most of the messages from people who died at their own hands were, like the Wimbledon messages, explanations and apologies. Typical was the man who had gassed himself and who came to his sister-in-law in the audience at Margate. He said he was terribly depressed. 'I had to do it.' Then he asked the lady to pass on a message to his wife.

'I caused such a disturbance,' he said, 'but now she's happy and she has all my blessing. Tell her I'm glad she made it. She still has my photograph and sometimes she thinks of me. Tell her I didn't do it because I didn't love her, but because I did love her.'

A very emotional message came in Bristol. I went to a woman in the audience and told her that I had someone for her.

'She gives me water and then a choking sensation,' I said.

'It was my sister,' the lady said, 'she took tablets.'

'It was the second time she took an overdose when she died,' I said.

'Yes.'

'Did she have a child?'

'Yes.'

'She's talking about the baby. She had it when she was very young.'

'It died.'

'She wasn't married then,' I said. 'Now she has the baby with her.'

'Oh, thank you,' the lady said.

'She wants to talk to her mother.'

'She's in Australia on holiday.'

'Has she been gone six weeks?'

'No, three weeks.'

'Is she going to stay six weeks?'

'No, eight weeks.'

'She keeps telling me six weeks.'

'She went to Australia for six weeks after my sister died.'

'Ah yes, she went to a relative.'

'Yes.'

'She had to get away because she blamed herself. But it had nothing to do with her. It was him. Who is she talking about?'

'It could have been her husband.'

'Well, she says to tell her mother that if she had listened to her more, she wouldn't have taken her life. She couldn't cope. There was never any money. "I just couldn't cope with it," she says, "but it was a silly thing to do, I realise that now." Now she's talking about him again. She says he didn't give you any of her things when she died, nor to Mum. Mum had to fight and say, "I want it."'

'Yes.'

'In the end, very, very reluctantly he parted with a bit.'

'Yes.'

'But nothing you could make any money on.'

'True.'

'She says in the end it was her fault. Mum told her never

to get involved with him. Mum said, "That's the worst day's work you're going to do." She said, "I didn't listen." '

'No.'

'She says, "Tell Mum I'm sorry. But I will talk to her because I'll try somehow to get in touch with her." She tells me she was older than you and was supposed to look after you, but you were more sensible than she was.'

'That's what she used to say.'

'She says you've got more sense. "You wouldn't have got hooked like I got," she says, "because I did get hooked, you know." '

'I understand.'

'She says to you, "Don't do it. Don't make the same mistake. That's just between us." '

Two days later I appeared in St Austell and shortly afterwards I received a letter from a lady in Falmouth. I receive literally hundreds of letters and I only quote extracts from this one because it gives the reaction of someone who had never seen clairvoyance or healing demonstrated before.

'I had never been to see anyone with your kind of gift before,' the letter reads, 'and I want you to know how impressed I was. I have never witnessed anything like it. I don't suppose you even remember anything about what you did . . . At this "show" (I'm sorry, but I don't know what else to call it) you were in touch with a young boy who had shot himself . . .

'Also, the way you helped the elderly lady who came on stage, riddled, I believe, with arthritis, was incredible. She walked off the stage like a five-year-old. Yet when she came on stage, she had a stick and her daughter, or at least someone, to help her walk.'

This lady was obviously impressed with the young boy who had in fact shot himself in the head, because she went into some detail in her letter. According to the tape, I went to the boy's aunt in the audience. 'I have a boy shot or killed,' I said. 'It could be a war condition, but he's not in uniform. I think it was in the head. He was young,' I said. 'Was he twenty-two?'

'No, seventeen,' his aunt said.

'He's telling me it was an accident.'

'No.'

'I'm telling you what he's telling me but he said he had tried to take his life before.'

'No.'

'Is the gentleman next to you with you?'

'He is with me.'

I then asked him if he understood the message, but he had no knowledge of a previous suicide attempt. I was quite clear about what I was hearing, however.

'Well, that's what he tells me,' I said. 'He said he couldn't make it. He got tremendous depression, but he shouldn't have had the gun.'

'That's true,' the man said.

'He tells me he didn't get the gun by legal means.'

'That's true.'

'He stole the gun!' I exclaimed.

'He didn't actually steal the gun,' the man said.

'Well, he took it. Same thing because it didn't belong to him,' I retorted.

'That's true.'

'He left a note, and he wants to get if off his chest. Now he says again he stole it. He says, "I've got to get if off my chest." And he keeps talking about a note.'

'Yes.'

'"I left a note" – or a message. Can you follow this?'

'Yes.'

'Oh, he's giving me such a pain in the head,' I said.

The boy then spoke to me about two days. 'Was it two days before you heard about him?'

'No,' his aunt replied.

'How long before he was discovered?'

'That same evening.'

'He said two days. Did he have the gun two days?'

'No.'

'He's talking about two days and I can't change that,' I said. 'Now he's talking about his father. His father's alive.'

'He is, yes,' the lady said.

'Was their some problem with his father?'

'He was parted from his mother,' she replied, by which I assume she meant that the boy's parents were separated or divorced.

'Because he says, "Two days, two days before, I had problems." Did he live with his father?'

'He could have had problems with his father.'

'He says they had a bust-up two days before. A row.'

'Yes,' the aunt agreed, 'but not with his father.'

'Did he live with his father?'

'No.'

'I can only tell you he spoke of a terrific quarrel, and he didn't really know the girl. Why is he talking about the girl?'

'Because he had a quarrel with the girl.'

'He said she wouldn't go his way.'

'No.'

'Do you follow what I'm talking about? There was some big problem he had.'

'Yes, there was another boy,' the aunt said, 'who went out with his girlfriend.' (The tape is indistinct at this point and I may have got the latter reply slightly wrong.)

'He's not very clear,' I continued. 'He's giving me the message in bits and pieces, but he left a note, or a message.'

'Yes. He left a message for his younger brother.'

'That's it. But not to his mother.'

'It was to give his money to his brother to go on holiday with,' the lady said. She told me that her sister had found the note on a piece of paper upstairs.

'He shot himself because he couldn't get what he wanted,' I next said. 'What a strange thing to say. Do you know why he shot himself?'

'He was afraid,' his aunt replied.

'Afraid of what?'

'Because he nicked this other boy with a knife.'

'But it wasn't dangerous.'

'No, it wasn't really.'

'He said to me, "That was nothing. I'm not talking about that."'

'No.'

'He said to me – come on, slowly – he said to me: "I was a tearaway and I had to have my own way, and that's all there is to it." But he said he wasn't bad. "I had a fight or I had a quarrel but it wasn't bad what I did to the boy."'

'Oh, no,' his aunt agreed.

'He said it was nothing at all to do with that. "I had this row and I felt what's the good of going on? I can't have my own way." There's some problem with his mother. There was also a problem with his father and he wanted to get right away. Who did the gun belong to?' I enquired.

'His half-brother,' said the aunt.

'Hasn't his mother married again?'

'No.'

'Because he's talking about the other part of the family.'

'Oh yes, the other part. She had to marry twice,' was the reply.

'She's living with someone, or she's with someone,' I said.

'No.'

'Look,' I suddenly said, apparently frustrated, 'does

anybody else know anything about this here? Only you two? Because he's still talking about his mother, and there's someone else in her life.'

There was no reply.

'Yes, definitely,' I said. 'The boy who's next door to you but one, what relation is he to you?'

'He's my son,' the lady said.

Addressing him, I asked whether he understood what I was saying.

'Vaguely,' he answered.

'This boy is getting so frustrated,' I told him, 'because I can't get through to you. Do you know anything about his mother?'

'Yes,' the young man said.

'He wants to contact his mother but he says something's stopping him because she's got some problem here but there's someone else in her life.'

'Yes, there is,' the young man said, and I must have wondered why his mother had denied this when I had put the same question to her earlier.

'There definitely is?'

'Well, I think so, yes.'

'So you know what I'm talking about.'

'I think so.'

'And your mother doesn't.'

'No.'

'Okay,' I sighed with relief, 'that's all right. No wonder I'm getting hot here because he said, "Quick, quick, quick, get it over," and he said, "I must talk to my mother." Now is his mother your mother's sister?'

'Yes.'

'Thank you,' I said. '"Thank goodness," he said, "because she's not had a proper message from me. She only thinks she has." And he wants to talk to his mother. Now he loved his mother and yet he couldn't communicate with her.'

The young man agreed.

'That's a terrible thing.'

'Yes.'

'Now he's talking to me and he's calling me Doris. And he said to me, "Doris, you don't know what my life was like. I couldn't tell my people and I was so lonely."'

'Yes.'

'"And that's what made me do many things I did." He wanted to be loved, you see. It's all very well, he said, for his aunt and uncle to say they loved him but, he said, who showed it to him? Do you follow this?'

'Yes,' the young man said.

'He's holding quite a running commentary now I've got you,' I told the young man, 'because he feels you understood.'

'Yes.'

'You understood him better than anybody else and you tried to talk to him and tried to explain to him in some way, or you would understand. He again says will you please tell his mother that he wants to talk to her, and he's still saying it was a mistake. "In one way I wanted to do it and in another way I didn't. I didn't really want to do it and I thought it wouldn't kill me. I thought it would make people notice me."'

This had been a very long message, made longer perhaps, as I later told the lady, because I did not feel that she had been as communicative as she might have been, necessitating my going to her son.

I was not in the theatre to be examined but if possible to help or bring comfort to people in the audience for whom there were messages. I cannot therefore have expected the next question, from the young man to whom I had just been talking.

'Can you find out his name?' he asked me.

Since he obviously knew the dead boy's name, the purpose of the question can only have been to test me, and I should have brought that particular episode to a speedy end. Instead I said, 'If he gives it to me, I certainly will,' and I presumably resumed contact with the dead boy because I started asking further questions.

'Was the boy he attacked called Alan?'

'I don't know,' the young man said.

'Alan is some connection of his,' I said.

'He's got a cousin Alan.'

'Now he's talking about David or Davie – no, it's Davis, and somebody called Peter.'

'He's got a cousin Peter.'

'I was clearly getting warmer. I had discovered two cousins in three names!

'And who is Richard?' I asked.

'That's the boy who shot himself,' came the reply.

What astonished the lady who wrote to me from St Austell, and astonished me too, was that having given her son the name of the dead boy, the boy's aunt should have put another question: 'What's the name of the dog he's got with him?'

Some people want to have their cake and eat it!

There was a much shorter message in Ayr when a woman who had killed herself with an overdose of pills came and said she was determined to get through to her friend in the audience. I went to a lady who recognised her former flatmate.

They had obviously had a very close relationship. The dead woman told me that she had been rejected. She had loved her friend very much but could not go on because, as she put it, 'it was all so indefinite'.

'She gave you a ring,' I told the lady in the audience.

'Yes,' she said.

'She wants you to keep it always because it was such a thing in your lives. You were everything to each other. You have her picture, a picture of you and her together. You have it in a case with other pictures.'

'That's right.'

'How old was she?'

'Twenty-five.'

'She says she was nearly twenty-six.'

'Yes,' the friend agreed tearfully.

'Why do you blame yourself?' I asked.

'I don't know.'

'She says no one was to blame,' I told the lady. 'It was her fault.'

In Preston a man came to me who gave me a sensation in the throat. I felt that he had hanged himself. I went to a woman who turned out to be his sister. 'He's talking about his mother,' I told her. 'I think she's in the spirit world.'

'Yes, he had a row with her,' the sister said.

'He felt unwanted.'

'That's right.'

'Your father's in the spirit world too,' I said, 'and your brother had a difficult time at home.'

'Correct.'

'"I felt that I didn't belong," he's telling me. "I never had any love shown to me. I wondered if I was adopted."'

'We all wondered that,' his sister said.

'There was always a bust-up, regularly, he says.'

'That's right.'

'Now your mother has come through,' I told her. 'Your

brother says that they have met in the spirit world and it's all
right between them.'

'That's good,' she said.

'He says you must forgive your mother. She had a very
difficult life. So did your father. "She was afraid to show us
that she loved us." He tells me he tried to kill himself once
before, but not by hanging himself.'

'That's true.'

'This last action: he hanged himself and jumped?'

'That's right.'

'Was it over some stairs?'

'No, on the motorway.'

'I just felt he put something round his neck and jumped.
He said mother never got over it but it's all right now.
You've had a very difficult time. You loved him, not only
when he was alive but since then too. You loved him but
couldn't do anything to help him.'

He then spoke to me about somebody called Mary Ann.
'Does that mean anything to you?' I asked.

'No,' she said.

'I don't know if it's Mary and Ann, two people, but it's a
connection with your father.'

'Oh, it's all right, Doris,' she said quickly, 'I know who it
is.'

Any further exploration of this message was abandoned
because the man went suddenly away from his sister and to
the lady who was sitting next to her. This sort of thing often
happens at my meetings and I am never sure quite what
part, if any, I play in the process. I do not know if the two
ladies had gone to the theatre together that night. They may
have been complete strangers, but I knew that the lady's
brother had not known the person sitting beside her.

He brought with him a gentleman in the spirit world who
belonged to the lady. I do not know how this man passed but

I describe his message because it shows how one communication can lead to another.

It became clear that he was the lady's husband. He said that life had not been easy for them. 'We had a big struggle,' he told me.

'When you first got married, did you live with your mother-in-law?' I asked.

'No, we lived with my father,' the lady replied.

'And you had to get away. Your father tried to tell you what to do and he kept his thumb on you.'

'That's right. The only way we could have peace was when we got away.'

'And when you got away your life began,' I said.

'Have you got two children?' I next asked.

'I've got seven,' came the reply.

'He's talking about two. Have you got two at home?'

'I've got one at home.'

'Well, he's still talking about two.'

'I think I know which two,' the lady said, 'his favourites.'

'Well, one of them's at home?'

'Yes.'

'And you have trouble with one of the children.'

'That's the one at home.'

'He needs a bit of discipline. Your husband says if he was there, it would be a different matter, but he's proud of all you've achieved. He's shown me a photograph of himself. I think you've got it in your bag.'

'I haven't in this bag, I've got it in another one.'

'Is that the brown one?'

'That's right.'

'He said the brown one. And there's another one and I think it's in your bedroom. He says, "She talks to me when she goes to bed at night and says goodnight."'

'That's true.'

'He says you gave him the best years of his life and he thanks you because it wasn't easy. "I've got to be very honest," he tells me, "and say I was a difficult man."'

'That's true.'

'Now he's saying,' I told the lady, 'there was a problem over money. "I know all about *that!*" he says.'

The lady let out a little shriek.

'The bit of money you've got,' I said, 'hide it.'

'I have done,' she said to the audience's evident amusement.

'You lost some money before and you can never get it back now, so make sure you put your money where no hands can find it. "I love my boys," he says, "but don't put temptation in their way." I hope you understand.'

I have been working now for almost fifty years but never before, I believe, during that entire time had I come across someone who had set fire to himself. Such a person came to me in Gateshead.

He was a man who had passed three years earlier and he went to his wife in the audience and asked for her forgiveness. 'I tried once before and I was stopped,' he said.

'That's right,' the lady agreed.

The man told me that he had 'gone to sleep', but I told the lady that I felt a sort of explosion in my head and a terrible sensation of choking. 'What did he do?' I asked her.

'He burnt himself to death,' she said. 'It was the smoke.'

'It wasn't an accident,' the dead man told me, 'I did it.'

'Oh, my God,' I declared, 'he set himself on fire. He said it was an act of vengeance. What a dreadful thing to say.'

'I understand that perfectly,' his wife told me.

'He's talking about the children,' I continued. 'You lost one.'

'Yes.'

' "I was just so lost," he says. It's as if someone dared him to do it. He said, "I had to destroy myself." '

The wife's response was interesting: 'He threatened to do it,' she said, 'and I said, "Go on then, if that's what you want." I was trying to talk him out of it in that way.'

'He poured something on himself,' I said.

'Yes, petrol,' the lady acknowledged.

'And he set light to himself. There wasn't much of him left, you know,' I said rather gruesomely, presumably before I could stop myself.

'No, there wasn't.'

This episode is horribly grim, and I apologise to readers who find it distressing. I have included it in my book not just because it is very dramatic and provides excellent evidence of survival but because it carries with it a message of hope for anyone in despair. In fact the man's very next words were: 'I destroyed my body, but I'm alive, I'm free.'

He then asked his wife not to be angry with him. He said he had limitations and could not realise his ambitions. 'He was very artistic, I think.'

'Yes, he was.'

'He loved to be on his own, to be free, and he thought the only way he could do this was to destroy his body,' I said. 'He says it was a destruction to his soul.'

'That's exactly the way he was,' his wife agreed.

' "Well," he says, "I'm all right. I'm sorry I gave you all that trouble. Forgive me because I'm fine now." And he says he's not jealous of you.'

'I understand that,' the lady said.

'He's telling you to go ahead because you've got a new life. And out of the blue he's talking about Italy.'

'I'm sitting beside a lady who comes from there,' the wife said.

'He says he's met your dad in the spirit world. He again

says that he's sorry he caused you so many problems and he wants to repay you. The children are lovely, he says. Thank you for being so good. You were always mother and father to them. "I did try," he says, "but I was never a good father to them."'

The man who had taken his life in such horrible circumstances ended with these words: 'I'm not going to say goodbye because I'll come again.'

The man about whom I have been writing still sounded angry at times when he was talking to me, as I told the audience, and I am sure that entry into the spirit world does not automatically remove our faults and our problems – but perhaps it is not too frivolous slightly to alter the well-known saying: 'While there is life, there is hope' to 'While there is death, there is hope.' In his case at least death brought him liberation of a sort and he was able to say, 'I'm alive, I'm free.'

Of course it hardly matters how one commits suicide. It is a terrible business whatever the method. The young boy who came to me in Birmingham had hanged himself only the month before and he told me that this was the first time that he had communicated. It is interesting that he was able to do so only thirty-seven days after passing.

I went to a lady in the audience. 'You are his aunt,' I said.

She was very emotional, not surprisingly so soon after her nephew's death. 'Try not to cry,' I urged her, 'he doesn't want that. It's so hard for him to get back and he doesn't want you to cry. He wants to talk to his mum. Who found him?'

'His mother.'

'"I had to jump," he said, "I didn't mean to do it." He was either twenty-three or twenty.'

'Twenty,' the aunt said.

'His life was a dead loss. He was a clever boy and couldn't

get what he wanted. He wanted a uniform and they wouldn't have him. He says, "There was nothing wrong with me, you know." Music was terribly important to him. He played the guitar.'

'Yes.'

'He made his tunes up. He used to play anything. Oh, how long has he been dead?'

'April 2nd.'

There was a gasp from the audience because this was only May 9th.

'Just recently,' I said. 'But why is he talking about the twenty-second or the twentieth?'

'That was when he was buried – the twentieth,' the aunt said.

'Oh yes, because he says, "I was there, you know, and I saw them. I wish I hadn't done it. Now I realise there were other things in my life."

'He had a girlfriend, but his mum said she wasn't the right girl for him. She said he ought to wait. He also has a message for his dad. He says that it's very important that he looks after his mother. He's talking now about the two children next door. He liked them very much and he felt so ashamed when they heard about what he did. He says, "It just came over me so quick. I just did it."'

'Why, Doris?' the aunt asked, almost pleading for an answer.

'Why?' I said. 'He says, "If you ask me, I just don't know. I had no problem, no troubles, no reason, but suddenly I felt I'm going to do it. I wanted to be a policeman and I couldn't get in. They turned me down."'

A lesser cause for suicide can hardly be imagined and I am sure the audience felt a great sympathy for the boy and his family.

'Now,' I went on, 'he's saying hullo to Sue.'

'She's the girl next door,' the aunt said.

'He had ideas of going abroad. In fact he had it all fixed up.'

'He was going to Germany,' said the aunt.

'But he thought, what was the point? It didn't matter now. It was not important. He wants you to thank his mother for her roses at his funeral. "Tell my mother not to hang around there," he's saying. "She goes and sits on the bed and says why, why, why? Well, I can't tell her why, but tell her please I'm sorry."'

I do not wish to plague the reader with too many examples of suicide, and I hope in any case that they do not make depressing reading, because if so, I have failed in my object which is to show that there is nothing final in this life.

I will end with one further communication which, despite the background, has a certain humour. At least it made the audience laugh at times, and I like to think that the people who have passed into the spirit world after taking their lives will not object if occasionally we can laugh as well as cry at their tragedies. I do not mean them any disrespect.

We were introduced to a very remarkable lady indeed who came to me from the spirit world while I was demonstrating clairvoyance in Hanley. I went to a woman in the audience who told me that two members of her family had taken their lives, and she was not sure which of them this was.

'Two suicides in one family,' I said. 'How terrible.'

Suddenly both dead ladies were there – the sister-in-law who had gassed herself and the mother who had taken an overdose of pills. But it was the mother who had the message for her daughter. The sister-in-law could not get a word in.

'Who's Frank?' I asked.

'My husband,' said the lady in the audience.

'Is he the gentleman sitting next to you?'

'Yes.'

'Well, your mother wants to talk to him.' Addressing the husband, I said, 'She thanks you for everything you've done for your wife, who's been depressed, and for the way you've looked after her. She said – oh, I can't say that, she doesn't mind what she says to you! – she said you were always backward in coming forward.'

'That's perfectly right,' he acknowledged.

'You're not scared of me?' I asked.

'No,' he said.

'But you were scared of your mother-in-law?'

'Yes, a little bit,' he said.

'There was always a battle going,' I continued. 'She was a bit of a Tartar.'

'Yes, she was,' he agreed readily.

'She didn't think you were good enough. You wouldn't get in an argument, "and I liked to have a bit of a fight", she said. "He wasn't my idea of a son-in-law. He used to hide round the corner away from me. That annoyed me. He didn't ever get into an argument. A pity," she said, "I did like a bit of a fight."'

The audience was beginning to realise that this lady was quite a character and a very formidable personality.

'You got on well with your wife's father,' I said.

'Yes.'

'In fact, she says you adored him. "I was so mad," she told me. "I was jealous of him. That's why I was so tough." Now your wife's father's come. He's very quiet and unassuming. He's quite different from your mother-in-law. Goodness me, however did they live in peace? He says the only way to live with her was to hold his tongue, but he did love her and she loved him. She was a good mother and a good wife.'

He must have remembered to hold his tongue again

because his wife obviously decided that she was going to do all the talking.

'You're wearing your mother's ring,' I spoke again to the daughter in the audience. ' "Tell her to show it to me," your mother's saying, "to show she's still got it." Ah, it's on your finger now!'

'Yes.'

'Mother says now you've got the best man in the world.'

'I know that.'

'And she knows that now. "He might not say too much," she says, "but in an emergency he's fantastic." She's speaking to him again. She says she didn't treat him properly.'

'That's correct,' he mumbled.

'Tell him to speak up,' his mother-in-law instructed me.

'She says she wishes you'd stood up to her more and told her where to get off. You used to complain but you never said anything to her face, but you've turned out to be the best son-in-law a woman could have.'

It may be worthy of note that people in the spirit world usually return to their loved ones on earth in the same guise by which they would normally have been recognised. They seem also to retain their personalities and characteristics. Certainly this formidable lady may have gained in understanding, but I am sure that her daughter and son-in-law in the audience were in no doubt who was talking to them.

'Your mother didn't have three husbands, did she?' I suddenly asked her daughter. I had to be careful because I thought any minute the mother would give me a clip round the ear.

'Yes, she did,' was the answer.

' "Of course," she said, "and I ruled them all – the lot of them!" She says she was right up at the front then and she was a very handsome woman.'

'Very, yes,' her daughter confirmed.

'"They asked to marry me, I didn't ask them," she said. "They knew what they were getting, and they got their money's worth, I can tell you."'

At this point the laughter that had been simmering in the audience burst out like a small clap of thunder.

'This lady is very funny,' I said, 'but she doesn't think she's funny. In fact she said, "What's funny about that?"'

This only increased the general amusement.

'I have to be careful what I say,' I went on. 'She may have had three husbands but she was also rather a lady for the gentlemen, she tells me. She was always well groomed – she's standing in front of me now and she's touching up her hair – and she says, "I was good at everything."'

There was more laughter. 'She's a case,' I said. 'She's come back and spoken her mind, and "You wouldn't have believed it was me if I didn't. But I have softened. Well, you've taken care of my daughter and thank you. She's been a bit of a handful but in a different way than me."'

Her son-in-law agreed.

I suddenly turned my attention to a girl in red, sitting with the couple to whom I had been talking. 'Is this lady your grandmother?' I asked.

'Yes,' she said.

'I thought so. She says you're the one most like her. There are no flies on you, she says. You won't be messed around and you too like the men. She says that's no secret.'

The young girl responded very positively and seemed to enjoy this communication.

'"She's a pretty girl, just like I was," your grandmother says. "Just give them the runaround." And she says God bless you all.'

I probably thought this was the end of the message but a

moment later I was saying to the lady in the audience: 'You've got another daughter. Where's the second one?'

'She's at home,' was the reply. 'I wanted her to come actually.'

'"What, at home doing nothing?" your mother says. "She should have come."'

I could use this powerful lady to bring people into my meetings!

CHAPTER 9

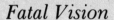

Fatal Vision

Deliberately to deprive somebody of their life is, I suppose, the ultimate crime, and perhaps that is why there is such a fascination with murder, gruesome as that fascination may be. What extreme circumstances impelled someone to terminate another's life? What sort of people were involved in the dreadful dramas that culminated in acts of murder?

To me all work comes alike. A message from a man who has passed peacefully in his sleep at the age of eighty-four may be as important to the recipient as a message from a young woman who was raped and left to die in a ditch. I am only the medium whereby the messages are transmitted, but there is no question of course that the dramatic impact is much stronger on an audience when the circumstances of death are exceptional.

I do not believe that I have any control over who comes to me. The spirits are always connected, usually directly, with at least one person in the audience when I work on stage, and I suspect that the urgency with which they seek to make contact may often have something to do with the circumstances of their passing. Perhaps that is why murder reared its ugly head on more than one occasion during my main 1985 tour.

A rather remarkable example occurred, however, a year earlier in Hull, and I am able to offer a brief account because my visit was reported in the Press.

When I went to Hull, I knew absolutely nothing about nine-year-old Christopher Laverack, a local boy who had been brutally murdered only eleven weeks before my visit. Apparently I was able to reveal accurate personal details that had not been made public at the time.

'I've got a child here,' I said, 'who has been killed in not a very nice way. In fact I think he has been murdered.'

I went to a couple in the audience, who turned out to be the boy's mother and stepfather. I believe that they had been invited to see me in the hope that I might be able to throw some light on the child's awful death, but I was unaware of this at the time.

'I find it hard to say this,' I told them, 'but he says they found him near the rubbish.'

'Yes,' the stepfather said, 'in a rubbish bag.'

'They do not know who did it,' I said.

'No,' was the reply. 'We can't find the murderer.'

'He was a very sensitive boy,' I said. 'I don't mean feminine, but in a kindly way.'

'Yes,' the boy's mother agreed.

'He is talking about March.'

'That was when he was killed.'

'He says they didn't find him for two months.'

'No, it was two days.'

'Who is Brian?' I next asked.

'I am Brian. I'm his stepfather,' the man said.

'I think his actual dad is alive,' I said.

'Yes.'

'But he does not want to talk to him.'

'No, I understand,' the stepfather said.

'The boy says, "Tell my mum I'm all right now,"' I continued. 'She's got a picture of him in a bag and one in a little purse.'

'Yes.'

'He says he's met Jim.'

'That may be my friend who has died,' the stepfather said.

'He died about two years ago?'

'Yes, he was a friend of mine.'

'He says, "Now I feel better talking to you." Who is David?'

'My son.'

'Now he's talking about Michael.'

'That was his best friend at school.'

It is obvious from the reports that the mother and stepfather were very moved by the message that the boy was all right, a message made all the more certain to them by the accuracy of some of the details that I was able to provide. The boy even told me that his mother had met her second husband by chance and that he was the best thing to happen to her 'since sliced bread', as he put it.

I have hesitated about using the child's actual name because I do not want to bring unnecessary distress to his family if they should chance to read this book, but because this was a well reported murder case I felt that I had to do so, because in any case they would certainly recognise all the circumstances. I hope very much that they can take comfort in the clear message I was given by the child to his mother that he was now all right.

I understand from the Humberside Police that the murder is still undetected and that enquiries are still continuing to catch the killer.

I want next to refer to the case of an entire family who had been gassed by the Nazis. The fact that they were unfortunate victims of a mass murder does not make their death any the less horrifying.

It was in Poole that I went to a man. 'Do you have a brother in the spirit world?' I asked.

'Yes.'

'Well, I've got your brother here. And now your father too. And good Lord, I've got Sara and Mary and Anna and Ted and Arthur and John – and they're all family! They're talking about the war. Someone was in a prison camp. They were chained up or something. Oh, I see,' I almost shouted, 'they went to the gas chambers. Five of them went together, all members of the family.'

I next asked about Anna, who the man said was his wife's aunt, and I spoke about Wilhelm, a watchmaker, who gave me information about a part of Poland that was now in Germany.

I was suddenly shot across to Israel. 'You've got relations there,' I said. 'Have you been there? Well, you're going, I can see a plane ticket.'

'Is your name Samuel?' I next asked.

'No, that's my father,' the man replied.

'Well, you're like him. Now your mother's come in. She says you got away. She's put a uniform on you. You were in the British Army. Are you German by origin?'

'Austrian,' he said.

'Your mother says to say hullo to Karl for her.'

'He's my cousin.'

'And Ariana. I think it's a Hungarian name. Now your father's brought a man who was a woodcutter. He's talking about the Rhine and he says he did business with him. Going back to the war, you had a very narrow escape.'

'Yes.'

'And yes, you were born in Vienna,' I said, 'and your mother loved dancing.' The mother then told me that she did not know her son's wife on the earth plane but she felt that she knew her well from the spirit world.

I ended with the following words: 'Your mother has just said that the terrible thing about going was that they just had to walk in and that when she last said goodbye to you, she knew she would never see you again and that was the worst thing for her.'

I hope it does not sound too facetious to say that the Nazis may have taken the lives of their victims but they could not destroy their spirits.

I think anyone studying the tape-recordings of my tour would be particularly interested in the meeting in Glasgow when two murdered girls came to me almost simultaneously, almost as if they were competing to deliver a message.

I know nothing about the actual events and I have not bothered to make enquiries, but here is what they told me.

One of the girls gave me a strong choking feeling, and a woman in the audience identified her as her son's girlfriend who had been killed in mysterious circumstances. The murder was unsolved at the time and the police were still investigating.

'There was a car,' I said.

'This is something we don't know for sure,' the lady stated. 'We've been wondering if she'd taken a lift in a car.'

'Yes, she had, I can tell you,' I went on. ' "I got in the car," she says, definitely. "I was warned never to do that by my mother, but it was late. Yes, very late. I couldn't get home and this man said he'd take me home and I got in." '

'Now I don't think she had been out with your son that night,' I continued. 'She was wearing a short skirt. A funny thing, I feel as if I've got no clothes on. She was found – in the ditch! "They tossed me out and robbed me," she said.'

For what it is worth, she had given me evidence that she had accepted a lift late at night in a car, that there was more than one person in the car and that she had been robbed and thrown out into a ditch. I have no idea how this fitted with whatever evidence the police had gathered. As I explained in my first book, I do not regard it as my function to assist the police in their enquiries although I would most likely answer any call for assistance. Catching criminals is their business, not mine, but I am sure that if what I revealed seemed pertinent to people in the audience, the information would have been passed on.

The girl gave me one further piece of evidence. She wanted to talk to her boyfriend, the lady's son. 'He gave her a ring,' I said.

'Yes, an engagement ring,' the lady confirmed.

'They found the ring,' I said, 'but she says not on her finger.'

The second girl went to a woman in a completely different part of the theatre.

'I have a young girl,' I announced, 'and I've got an idea that she too was murdered.' Listening to the tape, you can almost hear the hush that came over the audience.

'Just let me get this settled,' I said. 'This is not very nice. This girl was raped before she was murdered. The man hurt her chest.'

'That's right, Doris,' the woman said. 'Her mum's my husband's sister.'

'She wants her mum. She says she won't believe it. She says, "She won't believe I've come back." Was this girl twenty-two?'

'No, she was only fourteen.'

'Fourteen? She keeps saying twenty-two. There's some connection with twenty-two. Wait a minute, I've got it. She's speaking about the twenty-second. Who found her?'

'Her mother.'

'She says her mother's never got over the shock.'

'That's very true.'

'She says her mother would tell her not to do things but she had to. "I used to go where I wasn't supposed to," she told me.'

I was interrupted by someone walking in front of me. This is something that I beg people not to do when I am working because it breaks communication. It is like a wire being cut. I had some difficulty getting the girl back but I eventually managed it.

'Do you know who did it?' I asked the woman.

'Yes,' came the reply.

'Because she says her murderer was found and punished, but her mother would like to have killed him.'

'We all would,' said the woman.

' "Tell my mother please," she says, "to let it go. Just let it go, because he had one terrific mad moment." Does this make sense?'

'Yes, it does.'

' "He had one terrific mad moment and nothing can bring me back." She says her mother talks about her continually. "Tell her not to," she says. "Just say it's over and that I love her very much." '

This was rather remarkable and helpful advice perhaps from a fourteen-year-old.

I shall conclude this catalogue of murders with the story of sixteen-year-old Lynn Siddons which revealed itself to me when I was in Derby. Once again I use the girl's name because the case was so widely reported at the time. It comes to me with something of a shock that all the victims who appeared to me on my tour were young or very young, except for the family that had perished in the gas chambers.

According to the local newspaper, more than 1,600 people sat in stunned silence as this pretty sixteen-year-old girl, who had been asphyxiated and stabbed thirty times with a knife seven years earlier in a copse at Barrow-on-Trent, came with a message for her grandmother, who was present with two friends in the audience.

The case had attracted huge interest locally, and a fifteen-year-old boy had been acquitted of the murder. He told different stories about his possible involvement on different occasions. A statement he made on one occasion to the police that he alone was involved in Lynn's death was rejected by the judge as 'completely untrue'. Mr Justice May, who described it as a 'disturbing and odd case', felt that even if the boy had been on the scene at the time of the murder, he would not have been alone because he was hardly strong enough to have inflicted all the terrible injuries. On another occasion the boy claimed that he had acted under duress. During the trial, but not apparently previously, he suddenly accused his stepfather of the murder. It is only right to say that the stepfather categorically denied any part in the matter and said that his life had been made sheer hell by this accusation in court, and that no prosecution of the stepfather followed. Following the jury's verdict, clearing the young boy, Lynn's murder has remained the district's great unsolved murder case.

I can understand therefore in retrospect why the Derby audience was on tenterhooks when it became obvious to them that I had made contact with young Lynn Siddons. For what it is worth, she told me first that 'there were two of us together'. Exactly what this meant, I do not know. She then spoke to me about grass, and it is possible that she was referring to some grass nearby the copse where she was left to die.

'They killed me,' she said, emphasising the pronoun. 'There were two. There were three at first and the other one left.'

'I don't know about that,' her grandmother said.

'I don't like saying this,' I told the grandmother, 'but I've got to repeat what she said. "They took me to pieces," she said.'

'Yes, that's true, they did.'

' "I struggled and I fought and I knew I couldn't get away. Neither of them have been caught. The other one didn't do anything." '

I take this last sentence perhaps to refer to the third person who went away.

Lynn told me that her murderers would have to come to justice. ' "And I will see that they do," she said. "They shouldn't do things like that to people." '

'Did she sometimes call you Nan?' I asked, realising for

the first time that the woman in the audience was probably the girl's grandmother.

'Sometimes.'

'Who's Florrie?' I asked.

'My name's Florence,' the lady said.

'Oh, it's you. You're her grandma,' I said.

'Yes.'

'And who's Linda, or Lynn?'

'That's her name,' the grandmother said.

'Right,' I continued. 'Lynn shouted her name – Lynn, not Linda – and she said she wants you to know that they are going to pay. She didn't tease them, she says, she wasn't like that. They were just determined to get to her. Now I've got to be careful,' I said, 'it's almost as if I'm in the middle of a war. "You won't half get it," she told me, "because everybody knows who they are."'

'Everybody does,' the grandmother interjected.

'"And nobody does anything about it," the girl's telling me. "Thank God, Doris, you've got the courage to come and stick up for me. They all know who they are and they don't do anything about it."'

I have to say that whatever this may have meant to Lynn's grandmother or to the audience, it meant nothing to me. It certainly struck a chord with the audience, however, because they started clapping furiously.

Addressing the grandmother again, I said: 'Lynn says that the other mediums didn't know. Is that right?'

'Yes, it is.'

'She says they were afraid but I'm not. She says everybody knows, but I don't know what she means,' I concluded.

Lynn's grandmother has left no stone unturned in trying to bring the killer or killers to justice, and she has tried more than once to reach Lynn with the help of spiritualists, but she was kind enough to say that her granddaughter's message through me was the most successful that had so far been obtained, and she was convinced, from the details I provided, that it was genuine.

CHAPTER 10

---·~·---

How I See as a Psychic

The word 'clairvoyant' is derived from the French. The literal meaning is 'clear seeing'. It is usually applied only to vision beyond the normal – what I think of as 'soul sight'.

Gradually science is being forced to admit that the mind field is larger than, and possibly quite independent of, the brain.

I have explained elsewhere that I operate by sense, sight, feeling and hearing and that my knowledge comes from one or more of these faculties. It is not sufficient, however, just to see clairvoyantly. I have also to interpret what I am seeing. Those in the spirit world who wish to reach us often convey messages through symbols that they think will be easily understood.

I have always told the students I train that they must develop their own basic shorthand so that when they see these symbols they can quickly present a positive picture to the person who is seeking their help.

Clairvoyance is not achieved by everybody in the same manner. For myself, on one occasion I may see quite clearly, as with normal sight, and on another I have a sort of vision. Another time I may hear the voice, or there may be a combination of senses.

Clairvoyance can be divided into two forms – objective and subjective. Objective clairvoyance is when the personality presents a distinctly physical appearance. Subjective clairvoyance is when the psychic discerns interiorly as from the interior side of consciousness.

Psychics are often puzzled to account for the actual process by which they receive information and it is difficult to be precise, because it comes in so many different ways. I rather incline to the view that while practising clairvoyance, the medium undergoes a loss of individuality and becomes a different entity who works with a blend of all the sensory powers of consciousness in which past, present and even future merge into an ever-present panorama, in which reality stands starkly before us and all the petty incidents of normal life sink into insignificant background.

I certainly do not wish to make any exaggerated claims for myself. I know I have a special gift and I know something – but not all, by any means – about that gift and how it operates. I suspect that, although outwardly the same person, I become somebody else entirely when I am demonstrating.

To some extent we are all psychic, some of course much more than others, and have the ability to sense things. It is not something that need frighten us because it is entirely natural. 'Supernatural' is only a word coined by those who cannot explain natural phenomena, and there is a strong commercial interest in frightening people.

Fear of the unknown is very rewarding to those who commercialise it in books and films. I have known the unknown all my life, and what may be supernatural to some people is natural to me. I look on my work as normal, not abnormal.

Is a ghost supernatural? What, in fact, is a ghost? I could say that I see ghosts when I am working as a psychic, for I frequently see spirits who have left this physical plane. How can I see spirit, you may ask, when spirit is indefinable? If the spirit has no visible form, how can I describe accurately a person who has died, whom I have never seen?

When I work I mentally raise my rate of vibration, my awareness. I go into what some scientists call the 'alpha' – that is, beyond ordinary – sight. I do not see spirit as such because it has no form, so those who wish to make their presence felt produce for me a picture of what they looked like on earth. They quite simply think it and I am able to register their thought because I am like a television set that is able to reproduce the picture that is fed into my mind.

It is a question of a soul linking with the mind.

It is not just a matter of seeing what they look like, but also of understanding what they feel and what they wish to transmit to the sitter. It is an automatic process, almost like turning on a machine. I do not regard it as supernatural.

The clairvoyant of today is nothing new. In the Bible, when the king sent for his dreamer of dreams, he would have been summoning a seer. The prophets in the Old Testament all had visions. History is full of examples, like Joan of Arc, of people who heard voices. Perhaps they too had the gift of clairvoyance.

CHAPTER 11

A Funny Thing Happened

I have heard it said that we can only sense about thirty per cent of reality. If this is so, it means that seventy per cent of our world is shrouded in mystery. I have no doubt that, as time goes on, we shall come to learn and understand more and more about what at present is hidden from us, but it will be a long and continuing search.

I am the most ordinary of women in most respects. On the surface I suppose I am a typical suburban housewife. I may be a little larger than average, and I believe I have a good and methodical business sense, but in almost all respects I am similar to most other women from my position in life. If you invited me to tea, you would probably find that I think and talk very much in the same way that you do. If I am extraordinary because of my special gifts, I am nevertheless the most ordinary extraordinary person you are likely to meet. I have no false sense of my own importance.

I do not hesitate, however, to admit that I have been granted a very special power to see beyond our everyday reality, to look beyond it sometimes into certain areas that are unfamiliar to most people. This gift can be a burden, but I feel very privileged to have this special sensitivity, which I think is the best word to describe it. In fact I prefer the word 'sensitive' to the more frequently used word 'psychic' to describe myself.

In a way I am a sort of pioneer, I suppose, exploring the unknown. I have been given a gift and I believe that I was meant to use it. I feel rather humble about it and not in any way superior. In fact I have noticed that many of the greatest sensitives have been very simple people, sometimes quite uneducated and unable even to analyse their gift. It is just something one accepts.

Elsewhere in this book I have explained, insofar as I am able, how I operate as a psychic, but I cannot explain even to myself how and why I often see or feel things without making any mental effort. Why for example should I have felt uncomfortable when I was staying overnight in a hotel near the airport in Southend? I simply could not sleep. All night long I heard chattering and it seemed to be coming from a group of young pilots. That will teach me, I thought, to stay in a hotel by the airport. These young men obviously stayed up all night and had no thought for an elderly lady trying to get her beauty sleep. It was so bad that I left the hotel, although the management could not understand my complaint. I went to stay the following night in a boarding house in the town, and that night I slept like a log.

I recounted the experience to some friends who told me that the airport hotel was built on one of the sites from which RAF pilots had set off during the war to fight the Battle of Britain. By chance I had been sleeping in the hotel on the fortieth anniversary of the battle for supremacy in the air which saved this country from defeat. What I thought were airmen in the corridor were obviously in fact some of the famous few to whom we owed so much. Whether they were revisiting the scene of their glory or whether my mind was conjuring up events that had happened forty years before, I am not sure; but in any case I cannot account for how these sounds came into my mind. They just did.

Sometimes things just come into my head, perhaps when I am talking to somebody on the telephone. It is different of course when I am working because then I have to make a conscious effort. When I was asked to appear on *TV-AM*, for example, I could not just sit back in the hope that something would happen. I had to work as if I were on the stage. On one occasion, which was reported in the Press, there was another guest on the programme, actress Jenny Seagrove, who had made a big success in a series called *A Woman of Substance*. Her grandmother, who had died just over a week earlier, came to me. 'It was as if my granny was right there with me,' Jenny told a reporter. She asked me just one question – 'Is my granny happy?' – and I was able to reassure her.

On an earlier occasion I had agreed to talk to callers who telephoned into the same programme. It meant getting up very early, but all hours are alike to me when I am working. The first caller was a practising Catholic who was rather worried about contacting a clairvoyant, but following the messages she received, she told the thousands of viewers that she felt comforted.

'I work for everybody,' I told my audience. 'Hindus, Moslems, Jews, it's unimportant to me. I'm religious too. I believe in God and I'm a Christian, because I was born in a Christian country, but my idea of religion is living life to its fullest extent, helping other people and treating others as you would they treat you.'

'But it's a hard notion,' said the presenter, 'to explain to people who have been conditioned and brought up to believe death is a full stop unless your religion teaches you there is a heaven.'

'I don't quite know where heaven or hell are,' I replied. 'Astronauts have never found them. The spirit world is all around us. There is no heaven and hell. We make them for ourselves.'

There were two other callers on that occasion. The last was a lady from Buckinghamshire whose husband was in hospital with terminal cancer, the seriousness of which she had not revealed to him, when she herself had to go to the same hospital for an operation, also for cancer. Although they were only two doors away from each other, her husband died so suddenly that she felt that she had not had a chance properly to say goodbye to him, and she desperately wanted to do so. 'I feel it might help with the utter emptiness of my life,' she said, 'if I could feel that he was around me and close.'

'You've got over your own cancer,' I told the caller.

'Yes,' she agreed, 'as far as I know.'

'I certainly think your husband's around you,' I assured her. 'He knew he was going to die. Someone is telling me about the last holiday you spent together. It was very important. And it's a funny thing, you've done some rearranging with the beds. You've put a very big pillow right down the side.'

'Yes,' the lady said, 'I've put his pillow down the side.'

'And you lie in bed and you talk to him.'

'Yes,' she said.

The above example may not be very unusual in itself but it shows how, when confronted with any situation while demonstrating clairvoyance, I invariably am able to obtain information from the other side at will, in sharp contrast to when information comes to me uninvited.

A quite startling example of something coming into my head, with consequences I could never have foreseen, is the following story.

I am friendly with a photographer, who has taken many photographs of me over a number of years. He claims to be a strong admirer of mine as a result of something that happened seven or eight years ago. He was planning to bring over some pictures for me and a young man who assisted him in his studio asked if he might accompany him. The young man was about to leave for a new life abroad but had heard about me and wanted to meet me. Unfortunately the young man burst a Biro over his shirt and there was not time for him to go home and change, so my friend told him to fasten his jacket so that I would not notice the inkstain.

Later they were both sitting at my house, having a cup of coffee and checking through the photographs to see which ones I was going to choose, when all of a sudden, so my friend says, I looked up and said to the young man:

'I feel like washing your shirt.'

My friend's first thought was that the young man had opened the front of his jacket, but in fact it was still closed and the stain was not visible. They told me what had happened. Apparently I glared at my friend and interrupted him. 'Be quiet,' he tells me I said, 'I've got something else to tell him. He's going on a long journey.' In fact he was leaving only two days later to live with his aunt and uncle in New Zealand.

'Yes,' I said, 'you're off to America.'

'No, Doris,' my friend said, 'he's going to New Zealand.'

'I was pleased you made a mistake,' my friend later told me. 'I'm always pleased when somebody makes a mistake, particularly when someone is very clever, like you.'

Apparently I would have nothing of this and I glared at him again and said, 'Within five or six weeks, he'll be in America.'

They knew this could not possibly be. The young man had packed his deep-sea trunk and had bought his tickets. This was not long before Christmas. On Christmas Day, he telephoned from New Zealand to say that he was unhappy there and had not settled in at all. He called again in January to announce that he was coming home, but first he was going to visit America.

This little incident impressed my friend, who had hitherto sat on the fence, as he put it, where my work was concerned but who now believed in me. And this brings me to the story that I want to tell. It must have been three or four years later that my first book was published and my photographer friend read extracts from the serialisation that was published in the magazine *Woman*. He realised that they had never paid him for the use of photographs in the book which he had taken, entirely through an oversight on my part. He therefore quite properly got in touch with the publishers, who in turn got in touch with me.

I decided to telephone him. He was out, so I left a message on his answering machine, asking him to send me an invoice. It must have been six or seven months since I had last seen him, and in due course he wrote with a list of the photographs and the prices.

At the bottom of his letter he put a postscript: 'Doris,' he wrote, 'I have been missing some equipment from my studio over the last few months. Perhaps you could throw some light on the matter.'

I telephoned him at ten past nine on the morning I received his letter.

'Doris Collins here,' I said. 'Is that you, Keith?'

'Yes, good morning, Doris.'

'You'd better get those keys back off that chap,' I said, 'otherwise you're going to lose more equipment.'

My friend says that I went on to give him an incredibly accurate description of somebody I had never met but whom he knew and trusted implicitly. Over a period of about four months he had lost a lens to fit his camera, a fur cape, bridal petticoats, a bridal tiara and his camera body. It will be understood that he specialised, among other things, in wedding photographs. This was all secondary equipment, in other words not equipment that was used every day, and some of it was not missed immediately.

Knowing the number of people who used the studio, it was very difficult to identify the thief, and suspicion was at first directed against a cleaner and a young assistant. Never would he have suspected the man that I described.

He was a gentleman in his early fifties and a security guard to boot, quite the last person my friend would ever have thought capable of even borrowing such equipment.

He says I was relentless, that I had got it off pat. 'The man's fifty-two,' I said. 'He's got four or five jobs. He can well afford to repay you. And he's a transvestite!'

I must quote my friend's actual words: 'That was very interesting,' he told me later, 'because being a tranvestite, my petticoats would come in very handy, not forgetting the tiara and the fur wrap. I just visualised this chap, who at the time strangely enough had a beard, and I thought he would look a right so-and-so with a tiara on his head and a beard!'

My friend asked me if I was sure in my description. 'Oh yes, he's the culprit,' I said. 'Sometimes he has a beard – and he wears pointed shoes.'

My friend conveyed what I had told him to a colleague and to his secretary. It was true that I had described the man beyond any doubt in their minds as to his identification, and he had been given keys to the studio. He also wore a beard, shaved it off and grew it again as the fancy took him. But he was such a kind and pleasant fellow that they could hardly believe that he had taken the missing equipment. In any case nobody had ever seen him wearing female clothes or noticed any traits in that direction. Nor had he ever been seen wearing pointed shoes.

After some hesitation, they decided to call in the police and discuss with them their suspicions, without making any accusations. They said nothing about their conversation with me. By coincidence while the police were actually in the studio, the man who fitted my description walked in, and all eyes fixed on his very smart winkle-pickers!

Of course I am not saying that this man did remove the equipment, but it obviously disappeared during a time when he hired the studio, nor do I know if my information about his dressing in women's clothes was correct, but eventually my friend summoned him for the return of, or payment for, goods that were lost while the studio was hired out to him. Judgement with costs was eventually obtained.

My friend telephoned me within minutes of leaving court. I was pleased for him although I do not personally normally use my clairvoyant gift for this sort of purpose. It is for the police and the judiciary to pursue such matters, not for a psychic, but when I become involuntarily involved, or I am given information about such matters, I cannot help myself. Only independent evidence can vouch for the accuracy or otherwise of what I sense.

Two months later my photographer friend and I were talking about how I was able to describe a man so accurately over the telephone whom I had never seen. Did I get a vision, he asked, when I read the postscript to his letter, and then telephone him?

'Oh, no,' I said, 'I hadn't a clue until I telephoned you and you answered the other end. The picture came to me as we spoke. I could have told you more.'

My friend still laughs about the improbability of a middle-aged man with a beard, wearing a fur stole and a tiara. He says that two independent witnesses have since confirmed to him that the gentleman in question was a practising transvestite. How, he asks, could I have known?

And that is a question that I am not sure that I can answer, except to say that it is not always a question of concentrating to obtain information; sometimes it is put in my head.

Another extraordinary story is that of a dear American friend of mine called Ina Marx. I wanted to include this account in my first book but I was unable to check up on all the details in time. She will not mind my giving her name because she herself has spoken openly about these events to many people.

I have been going back and forth to the United States for over forty years. On one occasion I was asked to work for a yoga group in Connecticut, when I was approached by a lady who said she was planning to bring a group of people on a 'pyschic journey' to England. Some Americans are very fond of this type of tour, and I am sure they are very welcome to the British Travel Association. They go to such places as Stonehenge and Glastonbury, and on this particular tour they wanted to meet Harry Edwards, the world-famous healer. They employed me as a consultant to the tour, which included personal sittings with me, and I arranged for them to see Mr Edwards, who of course was well known to me.

The group stayed in London for two days to see the sights and do some shopping, and I visited them at their hotel. On my second visit I was talking to one of their members, a very famous yoga teacher, who had written books on the subject. She was a Jewish lady named Ina Marx who struck me as being emotionally disturbed and very ill. I was quite concerned for her. She has since become a dear friend of mine but at our first meeting she appeared far from friendly.

'I don't believe a word you're going to tell me,' she said, 'but since I have paid for a consultation with you as part of the tour, I'm going to sit and see what you can tell me.'

This was not a very promising beginning but I am used to this sort of reaction on occasion, so, undaunted, I persevered. In any case I made full allowance for her obvious distress. This lady was in trouble.

I told her that she had two daughters, which was correct. She had lost one of them to a religious sect similar to the Moonies, and this was one cause for her anxiety. Another was that she had separated from her husband who had been causing her many problems.

I learnt later that her husband was a millionaire but it was she who had set him up in business. When they were first married, she worked as a waitress to supplement their income. There had been a serious fire at her place of work and she had been forced to jump out of a window. As a result she received compensation which she gave to her husband. This was the start of his success. Among his many business activities, he owned the yoga school where his wife taught, and she was also worried that she might lose her employment there following their separation.

While I was talking to her, her father came to me from the spirit world. When I told her, she said, 'That's impossible, my father is dead.'

'He may be dead to you,' I said sharply, 'but to me he is very evident. In fact he's rolling up his sleeve and he's giving me a number.'

When she heard the number, Ina screamed. It was the number that had been tattooed on her father's arm by the Nazis before he went to the gas chamber. For a brief time she was quite inconsolable, but of course she was now looking at me with different eyes.

Her father was very definite in what he told me. The exact words were absolutely clear: 'Please do not let my daughter divorce her husband.'

When I repeated this message, she said: 'Why on earth not? After all, he's not living with me, he has another woman and there's no point in keeping on the relationship.'

'I can only tell you what your father says,' I replied. 'I can't tell you why, because he's not telling me. But he's repeating the message.'

Ina left the sitting a great deal happier than when she came in to see me. I had also told her that she would return to live in the house that she had left. She had quit the family house to live in an apartment.

Of course I forgot all about this and it was a year later that I was reminded of it when I was working again in Connecticut and Ina came up to talk to me. I recognised her at once and was pleased to note that she seemed a great deal better and happier. I asked her how things had worked out.

Despite her initial scepticism, she had clearly been impressed by the message I had transmitted from her father, so much so that she had returned home and told her friends that she was no longer continuing with the divorce. They all thought this rather extraordinary.

Shortly afterwards she was in a restaurant where she and her husband occasionally ate, and he walked in. He came straight over to her table and demanded to know why she had stopped divorce proceedings.

All she said was, 'I really feel I shouldn't divorce at this time.' She would possibly have felt foolish to have given the real reason.

This news was not to her husband's liking. He wanted a divorce, probably to marry his girlfriend. He therefore threatened her.

'Tonight,' he said, 'I'm flying to the Bahamas.' He had his own private plane. 'As soon as I return, I'll see my lawyer, and you'll find you'll come off very badly. There are ways and means by which I'll see you get very little.'

Her husband knew that Ina had no property in her name and precious little money. She only had what she earned in her husband's business, what little he allowed her, and some book royalties. The threat was therefore a matter of serious concern to her.

'I went home that night,' she told me, 'petrified. I thought, what have I done? Have I done the wrong thing? I'm going to come out very much worse by staying married than by divorcing him. I was very distressed and several times the next day I was on the point of calling my lawyer to tell him I'd made a mistake.'

She was woken that night by a call from the police. Her

husband had been blown up in his plane while trying to land on an airstrip in the Bahamas.

This dreadful accident changed her whole life. Everything was left to her in her husband's will, and some time later I visited her back in her old house to which I had predicted she would return.

I can only assume that her father knew that her husband was going to die, although possibly he did not know that the death would occur so quickly. It is a remarkable example of a man seeking to protect his daughter from beyond the grave.

CHAPTER 12

---〜〜---

The Importance of Relaxation

Today people all over the world cry out for the inner peace that can come from relaxation and meditation.

Stress is the cause of many illnesses. Many young people come to my meetings. They tell me that the old ways have not worked and they look for alternative pathways to lead them to tranquillity.

Often they fall into the error of thinking that there are short cuts to a higher state of consciousness. Drugs of increasing potency are used with the disastrous results that can be seen and read about daily in our newspapers.

A psychic needs no artificial stimulant and I am very much against the use of mechanical means to seek a solution to mental problems. Medicine is useful in many ways and I am a great admirer of the wonderful work done by doctors and nurses and all who care for the sick. I am, however, increasingly concerned by the widespread use of tranquillisers and strong addictive drugs to subdue the symptoms of mental disturbance.

Relaxation and inner peace through meditation have been practised throughout the ages by the wise. It is important to understand that love without power can bring a great deal of happiness, but power without love only produces tragedy. This is the message of all great religions. When love and power come together they can bring both contentment and emancipation.

When we begin to meditate, the first thing to realise is that negative forces, such as hate, bitterness and resentment, must be consciously discharged, and it is found helpful by many to use an image such as a peaceful scene or even a flower on which to concentrate in the early stages.

Do not lie down but sit comfortably in a straight chair, concentrate on the breathing, taking long breaths deep into the lungs. The important thing is to throw out the extraneous thoughts that will impede your progress at first.

You may hear noise, but in time it will be possible to transcend this. Eventually you will be able to walk into a room full of chatter and not even hear it.

Each day brings problems, often quite minor, but from time to time there arises a very major problem involving an emotional crisis that can cause a deep-seated disturbance. The practice of meditation uncovers suffering so that it goes back to the origin; and by going back to its root, one is walking towards the cure.

There will not be an instantaneous solution, so it takes time and much practice. There are no short-term answers to fundamental problems of life. People try alcohol and drugs as a means of conscious blocking, but this only obscures the symptoms of the disease while the real cause remains untouched.

Meditation attacks problems at the root, not on the surface. It is an ignorant way to seek a solution to problems by means of a material nature.

We are the lamination of our past, but constant dwelling on the past hurts, and the harping on old injustices is extremely harmful to present contentment.

In my family when one of the children complained of some difficulty, I would say, 'That's old history. Now is a new life.' The ability to throw off past hurts and live in the present is very important for a correct attitude of mind.

We all know the benefits of physical training but it is useless if we have a weak mind. We are not merely bodies, we must also consider the mind. Our actions are a result of thought and our thoughts are responsible for our actions.

Before starting, one should ask the reason for meditating. This is essential, for the foundation is purity of motive. It is to listen to the inner voice which comes from the fount of all wisdom. Most of the knowledge we gain in life has come from the words of others. We are influenced on every side by powerful psychological influences, often born out of the desire of other people to control our thoughts and movements. Many of these play on our emotions but it is the calm mind alone that can deal with problems.

In meditation we find time to shape our outlook and get a closer insight into ourselves.

We should understand that about a third of our mind is objective. This is the conscious mind that records impressions of our day-to-day lives. It is the ordinary thinking mind with which we hear, feel, speak, move or perform – conscious action.

The subjective mind is the compartment where we store the impressions of what we have seen and felt with the objective mind. Do you not see that the subjective or subconscious is a form of memory?

To reach this vast and powerful part, we do not need to concentrate. Instead we can let go and relax into a dreamlike state. Gradually breathing becomes quiet and time begins to stand still. At first about thirty minutes' meditation is quite enough until we learn to relax without any difficulty.

CHAPTER 13

Case History

'Would it be an idea to tell about this in your next book?' So wrote Coby and Frans Smits, a Dutch couple from Ruiga-huizen, following evidence I gave them about their son Robert. I think it may well be a good idea because their experience is unusually well documented. I have a transcript of exactly what happened, and they sent me three long letters and a postcard, in which they comment about my method of operation. I think readers may find it interesting. Mr and Mrs Smits wrote me separate letters on the same day, each recording in his or her own words what had happened, as they saw it. 'I hope my English is good enough to tell you my emotion,' Coby Smits wrote, and all I can say is that if my Dutch were one-tenth as good as their English, I should be very delighted.

'Frans, my husband, and I live in the north of Holland,' said Mrs Smits. 'We have three children. All three left the house some time ago, although the younger girl sometimes stays with us.

'Last year we had again a happy time in England, but when we came back from our holidays our son was not as he used to be. He worked on an old-fashioned sailing boat during the summer season. He suffered with pain in his hip. In September they told him he had cancer with no hope of recovery. You can imagine we had a bad time, especially during the two weeks when we still had hope.

'The 30th September he left the hospital. We thought he would like to stay with his girlfriend, with whom he lived together the last two years.

'Robert, however, preferred to stay at home with his family around him, including of course his girlfriend. So we telephoned his two sisters, who happened to be in Israel, that Robert was very ill and would not live a long time. They came home immediately.

'My husband and I stopped teaching. We all looked after

Robert, helped him as much as we could, talked about death and life after death. We had a difficult time but also a good time, being together so closely.

'At first we thought a diet could help him, but in the end we gave up. After six months he died.

'Robert always said to me that I must not be sad, that I had to accept, but I couldn't. I remembered the smallest details from the time he was a baby. I had to cry, I missed him, after all he had come back home again and we had nursed him day and night.

'I had to go to school again, which was pretty difficult, although everybody was nice and helpful enough. Then in July came our holidays. We always go to England, so we decided to try and get some relief there.

'I talked to Robert every day, not that I think this is wrong, but I got no answer. I only would like to know if he was happy.

'First we went to London for a few days, then we went to Malvern.

'On a Thursday morning we walked along by the theatre and saw there was a performance. We decided to go to the theatre that night but they told us there was a performance on Friday night, so we decided to stay another day, which was not in our plan.

'I asked the lady who was selling the tickets if she could tell me something about the play, because I thought *Clairvoyance* was the name of the play. She answered: "If you don't know, wait and see for yourself."

'So we bought the two tickets and went off to the Malvern Hills. That Friday afternoon I had the feeling that Robert was with me very closely but again I had that sad feeling.

'Then it was Friday night, 7.30. We went upstairs. Two seats in the circle. What a surprise! First your beautiful poem. Then I heard for the first time in my life about mediums, about "to pass over" instead of "to die". Of course if I think hard, I knew something about it. I had read about it, but all from a distance.

'Suddenly, Doris, if I may call you that way, you said: "I've got a message for two persons upstairs, but they've got to wait." My husband and I both had the feeling: She means us.

'After fifteen minutes you said: "I've got a message for a couple who lost their son with cancer, not so long ago. Does that make sense?" And we answered, "Yes."

'Then we got the most wonderful message which completely changed my life, made me happy once more, which I'll never forget.

'You got the word "Mutter", so you asked if we were English. We said, "We're Dutch."

'You told us how we lived in Holland, next to the grandparents, about Robert's special car which he wanted to give to his grandfather, about his two sisters, one of whom had to keep her hands off the car, about his girlfriend, about his plan to marry her, about his studies. "All those schools, and now all for nothing!" he said.

'Every message was as Robert could have said if he was still alive. We had put the car he mentioned in a special garage and we had already decided that his grandfather could have it if he wanted.

'But the most beautiful message came at the end. You said that Robert was happy and now believed in a life after death, and because all the other messages were precisely Robert's own words, as we felt it, we believed his message immediately. There is no doubt. We felt very, very happy. My sadness is away. If he's happy, I'm happy. So I want to thank you. I can laugh again, enjoy life again.

'I can't express properly how you changed my life.'

I have not quoted the entire letter and I have taken very

slight liberties with the wording in one or two places in
order to make its meaning absolutely clear.

The letter from the husband covered much the same
ground, so I will not quote it at any length. He speaks of his
son having come home to die after learning that a bone
cancer had spread throughout his body. He describes the
diet mentioned by his wife as being macrobiotic, consisting
mainly of cereals, vegetables, seaweed and beans, with no
meat, sugar, potatoes, eggs or dairy products.

'In the end,' the father wrote, 'Robert had come to terms
with death. He said that as there was no life after death, there
was nothing to worry about. He died quietly. He didn't
mind to die so young, he said he had enjoyed life as it came
and that he had had more than his share.'

Mr Smits went on to describe his own feelings at the loss
of his boy. 'I found it very hard to accept that he had died so
young. After all, he was only twenty-two, and as he was my
only son and I had a very good relation with him, I missed
him terribly. I didn't think that life was worth while and
discussed with my wife giving up our jobs and going to live
in a remote part of Spain.'

Mr Smits says that an extraordinary change came over
him when he visited England. 'After a couple of days,' he
writes, 'I changed completely. I didn't feel sad. On the
contrary I began to enjoy life again. My wife couldn't
understand me at all, and was very upset about this sudden
change.'

He describes their visit to the theatre in Malvern where I
was appearing: 'The next evening we went to the theatre
without knowing what to expect. I had a vague idea of
fortune-telling or something like that, but I was prepared to
accept anything. When you started to read that poem, I felt
very happy and that I had come to the right place and when
you started to give messages to people down in the hall, I

was very much at ease and pleased. When you said, "I have a message for two people up there in the circle," I looked at my wife and suddenly we both had a strong idea that you were talking to us ... and then we knew it was us.

'You told us a lot of remarkable things that were all absolutely true. Not only true to the facts but also true in the way our son used to talk to us, always making little jokes.

'You started by saying to my wife, "He calls you his Mutter, aren't you English?"

'We use for mother the word "Moeder", which sounds like Mutter, except for the "d" in the middle.'

There were other indications that convinced Mr Smits that I was really in touch with his son. For example, I told the Smits that they had two daughters and that Robert sent his special regards to Marie and told her to keep her hands off his car. 'We have two daughters,' he wrote, 'and the elder is called Anne Marie and she used to borrow his car, which Robert didn't like. You missed the first part of her name but you said "Marie" and not "Mary" and the intonation was perfect.'

Frans Smits then told me in his letter: 'When you had finished, we started crying, but not crying for sadness but because we were extremely happy ... Even if he would never speak to us again, we will not be disappointed.'

Later that year I received a postcard from Mrs Smits. In it she said: 'We feel less sad about our son Robert although we miss him every day. But now we know that we'll meet him one day. You must be very happy that you are able to give messages to other people, but it must be very fatiguing. So please look after yourself.'

Demonstrating clairvoyance and healing is an exhausting business. It does take a great deal out of me but I am a strong person, thank God, and I usually recover quickly. People do not always realise, however, what I go through. I do not realise it myself. I have to rest if possible before I begin work and it takes me some time to return to normal afterwards. Fortunately I practise meditation and I know how to relax.

Following my last major series of appearances, I was taken ill, whether as a result of my exertions or for other reasons I do not know – probably a combination of both. I have decided therefore that I will not again undergo so extensive a series of appearances, but as many readers will know, I have recently resumed my demonstrations all over the country. I discovered during the time I spent in hospital at the end of 1985 and the beginning of 1986 that I could function psychically even when I was sick.

I must have been delirious one night from the drugs I was given – for proper medical purposes – because I was quite convinced that I was due to take a meeting in Blackpool that evening. My husband and some of my family were in the room when I tried to get out of bed and get dressed for an engagement that was in fact scheduled for a fortnight later. It was all they could do to restrain me, so positive was I that I was due on stage, and I suppose that nothing takes precedence in my thinking over my work.

The doctor was called who assured me that I could not stand on my feet to take any meeting, and he promised that he would personally go to Blackpool to tell the audience that I was too ill to be with them. Only in that way could they put my mind at rest.

They made available a nurse to stay with me, and I remember that while she was stroking my head, a gentleman stood at the back of her and spoke to me. I told her, 'Your father is here, and he is telling me that you are his daughter, and that you are taking his ashes to put them under the trees tomorrow. Please don't take your mother as she is not well enough.'

The nurse was astonished. She told me later that her father had recently died and that she was disposing of his ashes the next day under the trees. So what she might in other circumstances have put down to delirium, in my case she realised was genuine clairvoyance. In other words, the sensitive has a part of the brain that communicates with the spirit world effortlessly, even when ill or drugged.

To revert to Mr and Mrs Smits, they both referred favourably to what they call a poem, which is a sort of little prayer I recited at the beginning of my meeting in Malvern. Since it had a beneficial effect on them, perhaps you may like to read it here. It is something I often include at the beginning of my demonstrations as part of my warming-up process. It is difficult to go cold into clairvoyance before a large audience but that is not the only reason for reciting it. I believe in its message and it helps to set the tone for what follows:

> Great Eternal Spirit,
> We ask a blessing as we meet together
> And I thank you for this opportunity
> Of bridging the gap between our world
> And the spirit world,
> And I ask most sincerely
> That whatever comes
> I may give with wisdom,
> Truth and honesty.

I want to finish this chapter by giving the text of a most extraordinary poem called 'Ashu's Advice'. It is extraordinary because it came to me while I was in an auto-state of consciousness. In other words someone else was speaking through me. I could never have written it myself.

I know a lady in Lucerne who is interested in my work.

She is a dermatologist and a practising Buddhist. She goes every year to Japan for meditation. When I was in Switzerland some time ago, she came to me for a sitting and asked if she might record what happened. I saw no objection, and apparently while in the auto-state to which I have referred, I recited a poem and said that it was being given to me by a guide named Ashu.

A year later this lady brought me a transcript of her tape, which included the poem. She had taken it to her retreat in Japan where the poem was received with great interest because the words were similar to those that a Buddhist monk might have used and only a Buddhist master would be likely to use some of the phrases. As for the name Ashu, it was not a name associated with Buddhism but turned out to be a Sanskrit name for a departed spirit.

Make what you like of this poem with its Buddhist connections by a departed spirit. It is Ashu's advice, not Doris's, but it appears that somehow I spoke these words:

We will see that your feet are well shod.
We will be there, when you fall, to give you a helping hand,
      to raise you up.
O, fall you will of course. Hurt you will be, tears will flow,
      because the call of the flesh will be very strong.
But you will win.

The fight has always been since a child within you, and it
      will continue. There is no other way for you.
So, go with the wind.
Where the wind blows, you will go.
Where the wind blows your seed, it will flourish.
Do not fight against destiny.

The years that you have spent in learning are not wasted.

You must go forward and go on.

But two pathways can be together.

The pathway of the enlightened one and the pathway of service is the same.

You want to divide time – do not.

Very few children come to this pathway with that knowledge.

Always they think there is a division.

Singlemindedness is important. Do not make that division.

Do not fight what is inevitable.

As I said, go where the wind takes you.

Where you plant your feet, there sow the seed in the ground.

Then you will go to other places, and plant your seed there.

There are certain people who have come to this earthplane with that knowledge.

And at a given time that knowledge flourishes.

They are called the teachers of the world.

Some are great, some are small, but whatever they do is for progress.

So do not ask if you are great or small because even the grain of sand on the beach is important.

It makes one whole.

And so my child you are as of God and you are part of that great eternal source of life, the Buddha, the Mana, the Christos, the God.

May he give you his blessing.

May he walk with you.

May he give you peace and contentment.

And above all give you courage, that you may be steadfast in your endeavours and rich in your reward.

CHAPTER 14

Life Is for Living

I have discovered that the main purpose in life is to be fulfilled. What this means only becomes clear as one grows in age and wisdom. The life that unfolds for a child is probably relatively unimportant. Then come the adolescent years which bring hopes and desires for the future. It is not usually before middle age that people look consciously for some purpose in life.

Every now and again one meets a person who somehow seems to have changed course during their middle years and become awakened to their purpose. They have learnt that life here on earth has a definite reason, and they find happiness and peace when they discover that life is a wonderful preparation for the world that we must pass to when we die.

I know that, although I always wanted to give service, it was not until halfway through my life that I understood how important this was to me. The people I met seemed to fall into a pattern that always led me in a certain direction, towards the work that is now so much part of my life.

I fully believe that through circumstances in our life we draw towards us the great power of thought – perhaps thought which receded into our subconscious years before but which comes again to the surface at a given time in our life when we are ready.

I know from my own experience and from talking to many dedicated people whom I have met that when we find this way of inner fulfilment, life is so full that we never have time to be bored or lonely and indeed there are not enough hours in the day to complete the tasks that confront us.

It is then that we realise that we can never live for ourselves alone, for every hour of every day we are touching somebody else's life, whether it be mentally or physically.

Let us try to be very careful that there is a constructive purpose in what we do, because in every life the weeds grow faster than the flowers. We must constantly weed our garden.

Not one of us is perfect. Life is a schoolhouse of learning and when we understand that, we know that death is not the end but a continuation of another way.

When I look back over my life, I do not think I would change one aspect of it. Like everyone else, I have made many mistakes and I have lived through both happy times and unhappy ones. I do not regret the unhappiness, although when I was passing through it, it disturbed me greatly. I know now that it had to be. Disappointment and sorrow, as well as joy and contentment, are all part of life and have a purpose. Could I help anybody who comes to me in trouble if I had never had trouble myself?

All experience makes one grow, makes one strong, forms character and gives one courage to face the future. Nobody need ever despair, because nobody is in fact alone in this world.

In this book I have barely touched on the real driving force behind my quest, and I have made little reference to the spiritual side of my work without which there can be no real development in the true sense of the word.

I am basically a Universalist, believing that there are many paths to God and that no one religion has the complete answer. All religions have much in common and they all teach us that we can reach out hopefully to the Life Force of which we are all a part, in the certain knowledge that good will triumph over evil.

Each seeker after peace, harmony and real development must cast out hatred and bitterness and try, above all, to be sincere and truthful. I hope that I have been able to achieve this to some extent during my years of working, although one should never be complacent.

I am a great believer in destiny. There are some who come

to this earth plane and never seem to find their true pathway, but progress is open to every soul and no one is ever left without a guiding light. However disappointed and unhappy we may feel, we can always lift ourselves up with the knowledge that the great Eternal Spirit is there within each one of us and is part of our living, our thinking and our very existence.

So those of you who have read my book and ask, 'Is this my pathway? Is this for me?', listen to your inner voice which is the fount of all wisdom.

If you decide to follow the path of service, you may find that the way will be hard and that you will lose many friends in consequence, but so long as your conscience is quite clear, it matters not. If you have a destiny to fulfil, the right people will be drawn to you in a miraculous way, and although you may hesitate at the crossroad, uncertain which direction to take, you will be shown the right path.

Many people in the course of my work have said, 'But yours is a religion that deals with death', and I reply that mine is a religion that deals with life! Living your life to its fullest extent will enrich not only you but all whom you touch. Every day, every hour, every minute we are touching someone else's life, whether in thought or deed. Perhaps it will even be you who changes the course of man's thinking.

The world today is in desperate need of spiritual awareness. It may be you to whom the responsibility will be given to help increase that awareness; and if so, grasp the opportunity, use it and have the firmness of purpose to tread the path your heart dictates.

It could be you who will inspire those who will follow, and when you pass to the spirit world, as we all must do, you may hear the words, 'Well done, thou good and faithful servant. The world is a better place because you passed that way.'